WORLD RELIGIONS

NATIVE AMERICAN RELIGIONS

THIRD EDITION

WORLD RELIGIONS

African Traditional Religion
Baha'i Faith
Buddhism
Catholicism & Orthodox Christianity
Confucianism
Daoism
Hinduism
Islam
Judaism
Native American Religions
Protestantism
Shinto
Sikhism
Zoroastrianism

WORLD RELIGIONS

NATIVE AMERICAN RELIGIONS

THIRD EDITION

by
Paula R. Hartz
Series Editors: Joanne O'Brien and Martin Palmer

CHELSEA HOUSE
PUBLISHERS
An imprint of Infobase Publishing

Native American Religions, Third Edition

Chelsea House
An imprint of Infobase Publishing
132 West 31st Street
New York NY 10001

Library of Congress Cataloging-in-Publication Data
Hartz, Paula.
  Native American religions / Paula R. Hartz. — 3rd ed.
    p. cm. — (World religions)
  Includes bibliographical references and index.
  ISBN 978-1-60413-111-6 (acid-free paper) 1. Indians of North America—Religion—Juvenile literature. 2. Indians of North America—Rites and ceremonies—Juvenile literature. I. Title. II. Series.

E98.R3H25 2009
299.7—dc22

      2008051197

This book was produced for Chelsea House by Bender Richardson White, Uxbridge, U.K.
Project Editor: Lionel Bender
Text Editor: Ronne Randall
Designer: Ben White
Picture Researchers: Joanne O'Brien and Kim Richardson
Maps and symbols: Stefan Chabluk

Printed in China

CP BRW 10 9 8 7 6 5 4 3 2 1

This book is printed on acid-free paper.

CONTENTS

PREFACE

Almost from the start of civilization, more than 10,000 years ago, religion has shaped human history. Today more than half the world's population practice a major religion or indigenous spiritual tradition. In many 21st-century societies, including the United States, religion still shapes people's lives and plays a key role in politics and culture. And in societies throughout the world increasing ethnic and cultural diversity has led to a variety of religions being practiced side by side. This makes it vital that we understand as much as we can about the world's religions.

The World Religions series, of which this book is a part, sets out to achieve this aim. It is written and designed to appeal to both students and general readers. The books offer clear, accessible overviews of the major religious traditions and institutions of our time. Each volume in the series describes where a particular religion is practiced, its origins and history, its central beliefs and important rituals, and its contributions to world civilization. Carefully chosen photographs complement the text, and sidebars, a map, fact file, glossary, bibliography, and index are included to help readers gain a more complete understanding of the subject at hand.

These books will help clarify what religion is all about and reveal both the similarities and differences in the great spiritual traditions practiced around the world today.

Areas where Native American religions can be found

© Infobase Publishing

CHAPTER 1

INTRODUCTION: THE SACRED WAY

Each year in June, when the Sun is highest in the sky, holy men of the Lakota Nation of the western plains choose a special sacred place in the countryside. The area, which changes every year, must be large and open, away from buildings that detract from the purity of the landscape. Sagebrush and cottonwood trees must grow nearby. When the holy men have chosen a site, they perform the complex rituals necessary to sanctify the land for the Sun Dance, a Lakota ceremony for world renewal.

At the appointed time hundreds of members of the Lakota Nation, many of whom have traveled great distances for the ceremony, gather at the site to participate in or observe the four-day ritual of the Sun Dance. In the Lakota religion, people understand themselves to be a part of the cycle of all life. The Sun Dance reminds them of their sacred origins and the necessity of living in harmony with the rhythms of the Earth to maintain balance and order in the universe. It is an important part of Lakota culture, one of seven sacred ceremonies that the Lakota believe were brought to their people by Buffalo Calf Woman, a spirit messenger.

A group of Lakota Sioux in traditional dress outside Rosebud Indian Reservation, Arkansas. Each Native American tribe has its own distinct customs, beliefs, and languages closely bound to the Earth and the environment in which they live.

TRADITIONAL HOMELANDS OF MAJOR NATIVE AMERICAN GROUPS, CA. 1700–1800s

Northwest Coast
Above the Columbia River, along the Pacific Coast to southern Alaska

Bella Bella
Bella Coola
Chinook
Coast Salish:
    Chehallis
    Nisqually
    Puyallup
    Quinanet
    Squaxin
Eyah
Haida
Kwakiutl
Nootka

Quileute
Tillamook
Tlingit
Tsimshian

California
California Coast

Achumauii
Alsoyewi
Cahuilla
Chumash
Costano
Hupa
Ipai
Karok
Luiseño
Maidu
Miwok

Monache
Pomo
Shasta
Tipai
Wappo
Wintum
Yana
Yokut
Yurok

Subarctic
Canada and Alaska below the Arctic Circle

Anishinabe
    (Chippewa/
     Northern Ojibwa)
Beaver
Carrier

Chilcotin
Chipewyan
Cree
Dogrib
Han
Hare
Ingalik
Kaska
Koyukon
Kutchin
Montagnais
Naskapi
Sarcee
Sekani
Slave
Tanaina
Tutchone
Yellowknife

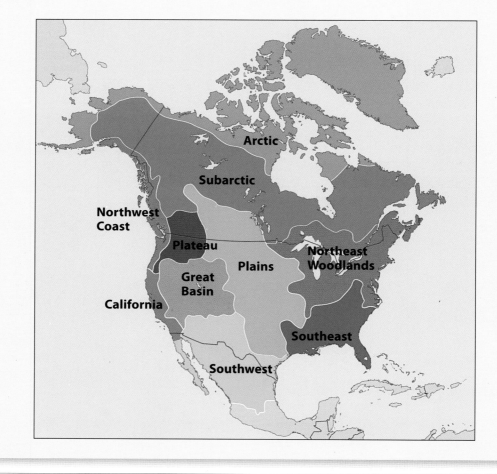

Plateau

From the Cascade Range in northwestern Canada, south to the Sierra Nevada

Cayuse
Coeur d'Alene
Flathead
Kalispel
Klamath
Kutenai
Lillooet
Modoc
Nez Perce
Nicola
Okanagan
Palouse
Sanpoil
Shuswap
Spokane
Thompson
Umatilla
Walla Walla
Wanapam
Yakima

Great Basin

Desert region, including Nevada and parts of Utah, California, Idaho, Wyoming, and Oregon

Bannock
Goshute
Kawaiisu
Paiute
Shoshone
Ute
Washo

Southwest

An area that includes Arizona, New Mexico, southern Utah, parts of Texas and northern Mexico

Apache:
    Chiricahua
    Cibecue
    Jicarilla
    Lipan
    Mescalero
    Mimbreño
    San Carlos
    Tonto
    White Mountain
Coahuiltec
Cocopa

Havasupai
Jumeño
Karenkawa
Maricopa
Mayo
Mojave
Navajo
Pima
Pueblo:
    Hopi
    Keres
    Tano
    Tewa
    Northern Tiwa
    Southern Tiwa
    Towa
    Zuni
Quechan
Seri
Tarahumara
Tehueco
Tepecano
Tepehuan
Tohono O'odham
    (Papago)
Walapai
Yaqui
Yavapai

Plains

Canada to southern Texas; Mississippi River, west to the Rocky Mountains

Arapaho
Ankara
Assiniboine
Blackfoot:
    Blood
    Gros Ventre
    Piegan
    Sarcee
    Sikiska (Northern
    Blackfoot)
Cheyenne
Comanche
Crow
Hidatsa
Iowa
Kansa
Kiowa
Kiowa-Apache
Lakota (Sioux):
    Santee
    Teton
    Yankton
    Yanktonai
Mandan

Missouri
Omaha
Osage
Oto
Pawnee
Ponca
Quapaw
Tonkawa
Wichita

Northeast Woodlands

Nova Scotia and Maine, west to Minnesota, south to Kentucky

Abnaki
Algonquin
Anishinabe
    (Chippewa/
    Ojibwa)
Beothuk
Delaware (Lenape):
    Munsee
    Unalachtigo
    Unami
Erie
Fox (Mesquakie)
Huron
Illinois
Iroquois:
    Cayuga
    Mohawk
    Onondaga
    Oneida
    Seneca
    Tuscarora
Kickapoo
Mahican
Maliseet
Massachuset
Menominee
Miami
Micmac
Mohegan
Nanticoke
Narraganset
Neutral
Ottawa
Pequot
Potawatomi
Powhatan
Sauk
Shawnee
Susquehanna
Wampanoag
Winnebago

Southeast

Carolinas to southern Florida, west to Texas

Ais
Alabama
Apalachee
Atakapa
Caddo
Calusa
Catawba
Cherokee
Chickasaw
Chitimacha
Choctaw
Coushatta
Creek
Hitchiti
Lumbee
Natchez
Seminole
Timucua
Tunica
Yamasee
Yazoo
Yuchi

Arctic

Arctic Circle area

Aivilik Inuit
Aleut
Baffinland Inuit
Bering Strait Inuit
Caribou Inuit
Copper Inuit
East Greenland Inuit
Iglulik Inuit
Labrador Inuit
Mackenzie Inuit
Netsilik Inuit
North Alaskan Inuit
Pacific Yuit
Polar Inuit
Southwest Alaskan
Inuit
West Greenland Inuit

The Lakota Sun Dance is only one of many similar rituals performed by peoples of the Great Plains, the vast grassland region of central North America, and only one of hundreds of religious ceremonies that Native peoples conduct throughout North America. For 75 years at the end of the 19th century and the beginning of the 20th, it was illegal for Native Americans in the United States and Canada to observe their religious ceremonies. The survival of the Sun Dance ceremony and of many other ceremonies shows the determination of Native Americans to preserve and practice their religions, even in the face of opposition.

THE HISTORY OF NATIVE AMERICAN RELIGIONS

Long before European explorers reached North American shores, the land was home to hundreds of groups of Native Americans. These native peoples lived in villages that dotted the North American continent, sustaining themselves by hunting, fishing, and farming. It has been estimated that in the 1600s, before contact with European cultures, well over 1 million Native Americans were living in North America north of what is now the Mexican border, the area covered in this book.

LANGUAGE AND COMMUNICATION

Each tribe was distinct and different from the others. For one thing, each spoke its own language. Although some neighboring tribes might have languages similar enough that people could understand each other, that was not always the case. Native Americans spoke languages that were in places as different from one another as, for example, English and Hungarian. Scholars estimate that at one time there may have been 2,200 different Native American languages, and they have identified seven different language families among the Indians of the Plains alone. In that area, where tribes with very different languages often met, they developed a sign language, a kind of international code that enabled them to communicate. In addition to speaking different languages, each tribe had its own culture and customs and its own way of building homes and making clothing and everyday objects such as tools, weapons, and utensils. Each tribe also had its own set of beliefs and religious practices closely associated with its particular culture.

NATIVE AMERICAN RELIGIONS

There is no single "Native American religion." Similarities can be found among native religions, just as similarities can be found between Christianity and Islam or between Daoism and Buddhism, but the religious customs of different tribes can be and are quite varied.

Native American religions differ from "organized" religions in several ways. They are not "systematic." In other words, they have no church buildings and no church hierarchy or organizational structure. Although some tribal tales recall the deeds of famous tribe members, most Native American religions do not rely on central historical figures such as Moses, Jesus, or Buddha, and they are more strongly tied to nature and its rhythms than to individual historic events.

AN ORAL TRADITION

Traditional Native American culture has always been oral, with information passed down by word of mouth. There is no written set of beliefs, no "rules" that "followers" must adhere to. There is no holy book, such as the Bible or Quran. In many ways Native American spirituality is similar to other religions with folk roots, such as Shinto or Daoism. The fact that there is no written creed does not suggest that there were no standards of behavior or ethics, however. Strict rules for living a decent and ethical life governed all Native American cultures. Tribe members were taught by example, and those guiding principles were not memorized in formal lessons but were internalized from childhood and became a part of daily life.

COMPLEX BELIEFS

When European settlers first came into contact with Native peoples, the differences they saw led them to conclude that the Indians

An Alaskan bald eagle in flight. Flying higher than any other bird, the eagle embodies a strong spiritual presence, one that communicates between Earth and the most powerful forces of the universe. Eagle feathers are used ritually by many tribes to invoke the bird's spirit power.

had no religion, or at least no "real" religion. The Native Americans they met had no written language so there were no books from which the newcomers might learn about Native religions. In addition, few non-Indians bothered to learn Native American languages, and the Native Americans often deliberately excluded the outsiders from their holiest rituals. Not until the early years of the 20th century did people finally begin to examine Native American belief systems. They found that far from being a simplistic form of "nature worship," Native American beliefs were often rich, deep, and complex.

In recent years, as knowledge of Native American customs has become more widespread, so has respect for their religious traditions. Many Native Americans have returned to their roots, seeking spiritual renewal in traditional rituals and practices. Ceremonies for purification and healing, for celebrating the cycles of nature, and for renewing the land attract participants and observers from many backgrounds, those people who find the ceremonies and celebrations spiritually meaningful.

BASIC CONCEPTS

Although the ways of expressing spiritual belief vary widely from region to region and tribe to tribe, certain basic concepts or ideas do occur in most Native American religions.

- Great Spirit: A Great Power, sometimes called Great Spirit or Great Mystery (Wakan Tanka, Manitou, Orenda, among other names) underlies all creation. This power is not a personal god, such as the Judeo-Christian God, and it cannot be imagined in human form. Rather it is a universal force to which all of nature is attuned. All of nature, including human nature, is the creation of this Great Power.
- Spirits in the universe: All things in the universe are alive and contain spirit within them. Spirit forces actively affect human lives in ways that can be both good and bad. The Earth, which nourishes and sustains life, and to which people return after death, is particularly endowed with spirit and is to be respected and revered. All forms of life interact and depend on all others.
- Walk in the sacred way: The individual is called on to "walk in the sacred way"—that is, to live in balance and harmony with the universe and the spirit world. People find their own sacred way by seeking clues to the sacred in dreams and visions.
- Oral tradition and ceremonies: Values, beliefs, morals, ethics, and sacred traditions are passed on through an oral tradition and through ceremonies. Cultural bonding takes place through rituals developed by each group over centuries. These often include dancing, singing, drumming, and feasting, as well as purification rites, fasting, and physical ordeals.

- Medicine men and women: Certain people (sometimes called shamans, medicine men or women, or singers) have special ties to the higher powers. Their special calling enables them to mediate between the spirit world and the Earthly world for healing, spiritual renewal, and the good of the community.
- Humor: Humor is a part of the sacred way because people need to be reminded of their foolishness.

ORIGINS OF NATIVE AMERICAN RELIGIONS

Native American religions go back to distant prehistory. Scholars who study ancient cultures believe that the ancestors of the Native Americans may have migrated to the North American continent from Asia more than 12,000 years ago, traveling across a land bridge that once linked Siberia to Alaska across what is now the Bering Strait. These peoples moved in bands, or tribes,

Ancient Native American cave paintings in Arizona. In their myths, many tribes tell of a time when there was no difference between animals and humans who spoke the same language. The prehistoric Native American civilization centered around the present-day Four Corners area of the southwest United States that emerged around 1200 B.C.E.

gradually spreading south and east across North America. These first Americans probably brought their religious beliefs with them, gradually adapting them to the environment they settled.

SHAMANISM

In Native American religions students of prehistory find a continuous thread of shamanism, humankind's "oldest religion," in which mediation between the visible and spirit worlds is brought about by shamans. Shamans, or holy people, are healers and interpreters of the will of the spirit world, and shamanism is one of the earliest traceable forms of religion. Another feature of shamanism was animism, the belief that all things contain spirit, or life. This was a distinctive feature of Native American religion.

LINKS WITH ASIA

Scholars point to religious similarities between the Siberian tribes of Asia and the Inuit tribes of Canada and Alaska. The parallels they find suggest that these religions have common origins. Native American religions also share ideas—particularly about the importance of balance and harmony with the universe—with Asian religions such as Daoism and Confucianism, which developed in ancient China out of the same religious roots, and with Shinto, the native religion of Japan, which had the same Asian influences.

NATIVE AMERICANS TODAY

Approximately 4 million people living in the United States and Canada identify themselves as Native Americans. What makes someone a Native American is a matter of both heritage and law. Some tribal groups, such as the Cherokee, admit to full tribal membership anyone who can

CREATION STORIES

The traditions of Native peoples themselves often hold that their tribes originated in their ancestral lands and spread outward from there. The Navajo, for example, point to a place in the mountains of southeastern Colorado where the First People emerged from the underworld and began to create life on this Earth. Similarly, the Umatilla of eastern Washington State hold that their people were created in that place and have been there since the beginning of time. The creation stories of most Native Americans support their beliefs that they have always been in North America, connected to and part of the land.

At Wind River Reservation in Wyoming, a father helps his young son dress in traditional costume for a powwow, a gathering of Native American tribes, to talk, dance, sing, and socialize. It offers an opportunity for tribes to celebrate their culture and can vary in length from one to several days.

trace any Cherokee ancestry; other tribes admit only those who are at least one-quarter or one-eighth Native American by blood; still other tribes have other rules governing tribal membership.

The Native peoples who live on tribal lands, such as the Hopi and the Navajo in the southwestern United States and the Inuit peoples in Alaska and Canada, are most likely to have preserved the religious practices of their forebears and continued their religious traditions. Most people who declare themselves to be Native American, however, whether they live on reservations or in cities, do follow at least some Native American cultural and religious practices and attempt to pass on their culture and sacred history to the next generation.

ONE SACRED WAY

Native Americans do not segment their lives into the secular and the religious. Their culture and their religion are one, so closely united that many Native American languages have no word for *religion*. All work is considered prayer. A woman making a basket may pray to the spirit of the grass as she cuts it. Later the designs she weaves into the basket may have symbolic meaning. The art of basketry itself is a kind of spiritual gift for which to be grateful. The successfully completed basket, too, a work of both beauty and usefulness, is an occasion for thanks. Thus even a common utensil has a sacred dimension. Hunters and farmers invoke the spirits of game and fertility so that their efforts and the outcome of their labors will be blessed. Ideally people live with a constant awareness of the spirit world around them and act in ways that honor this awareness.

A SACRED POWER

Although they do not separate their religion from their everyday existence, Native Americans have traditionally believed in a higher power that created and informs all of life, and they have followed traditions and rituals meant to connect humans with that power, the basic tenet of all religions. Whether their traditions came with them from another continent or sprang from American soil, the religions of Native peoples represent an ancient tradition of deep spirituality.

CHAPTER 2

THE SPIRIT WORLD AND THE SACRED WAY

The Algonquins speak of Manitou, the Iroquois of Orenda, and the Lakota of Wakan Tanka, words usually translated as "Great Spirit" or "Great Mystery." These words all refer to the indefinable power that underlies all creation. However else their traditions may vary, almost all Native American peoples believe in a great sacred force from which all things come and which keeps the universe in motion.

THE GREAT SPIRIT

When Native peoples first came in contact with European religions they recognized parallels between the white man's God and their Great Spirit, and some groups incorporated the notion of a personal god into their beliefs. However traditionally the Great Spirit is not a supreme being, such as the Judeo-Christian God or

Speaking Rock, the left-hand column, and Spider Rock, the right-hand column, in Canyon de Chelly National Monument in Arizona are sacred sites for the Navajo people. Spider Rock is the traditional home of Spider Woman, a legendary holy person who taught the Navajo the art of weaving. Canyon de Chelly is unique among national park service units as it is composed entirely of Navajo tribal trust land.

Islam's Allah, who speaks to humankind. It is more like the Dao of Daoism, an immense and universal power that is above and in all things. The words *Wakan Tanka,* for example, literally mean "most sacred," and when people speak of Wakan Tanka they are more likely to be speaking of the sacred power of the universe rather than of a personal god formed by imagination.

The Great Spirit cannot be seen or touched, but it is present in the cycles and visible signs of nature. People can find evidence of it in the continuing change of seasons; in day and night; growth and death; and in the movement of the Sun, Moon, and stars.

People traditionally learned about the Great Spirit, or Great Mystery, through oral tradition, the tales of magical beings and important events and ancestors passed down from one genera-

Ancient rock paintings of humanlike figures with earrings and headdresses. The figures are believed to represent spirits that can be found in all things that have life, from the sky, Sun, and wind to the smallest of creatures.

tion to the next. They also experience this mysterious power directly through dreams and visions. Children learn from an early age to pay attention to their dreams and to examine them for meaning. They learn to be aware of the spirit world, which is all around them, a kind of parallel universe that is always close at hand. Later in life they may actively seek a vision for spiritual guidance through periods of fasting and self-denial.

THE CREATOR

Although all things come from the Great Spirit, the Great Spirit is not the creator of the world. In Native American belief that function is performed by a supernatural being with special creative powers, a being whom scholars call a culture hero. This being may have human form, such as First Man and First Woman of the Navajo, World-Maker of the Yakima, or Earth Starter of the Ojibwa, or a dual human-animal form, such as Raven of the Northwest or Coyote of the western plains. In addition to creating the world and placing humans on it, he or she gives the first human beings the ceremonies and cultural institutions that they will use on Earth.

THE WORLD OF SPIRITS

A central concept of Native American religions is the idea that everything in the world that can be seen or touched is alive with spirit or breath. All of the environment has a life. The water that comes out

Wakan Power

The most wonderful things which a man can do are different from the works of nature. When the seasons changed, we regarded it as a gift from the Sun, which is the strongest of all the mysterious wakan powers . . . We cannot see the thunder, and we say it is wakan, but we see the lightning and we know that the thunder and the lightning are a sign of rain, which does good to the earth. Anything which has a similar power is wakan, but above all is the Sun, which has the most power of all...

—Anonymous, Teton Sioux

(In Peggy V. Beck, *Sacred: Ways of Knowledge, Sources of Life.*)

Teton Sioux Prayer

Wakan Tanka
when I pray to him
heard me
whatever is good
he grants me

—sung by Lone Man

(In Alan R. Velie, *American Indian Literature, an Anthology.*)

of the earth is alive, as are the rocks and the hills. Each comes from the Earth, which is itself alive and revered as the mother—or, as some say, grandmother—of all. The spirit of the air can be felt in a breath of wind and the sound of the breeze as it moves through the leaves. The spirit of the rain can be felt in moisture on the earth. The spirits of rocks, trees, grass, wind, and rain cannot be seen, but they are a constant reality, influencing all aspects of human life.

The spirits of the dead may live as ghosts on Earth or may be reborn as animals. Ghosts are potentially dangerous, however, and are to be avoided for the harm they can do.

SKY SPIRITS

Many people shared the belief that the Milky Way, the broad band of faint light that can be seen in the night sky, was a "path of souls" to which people went after death. The Luiseño of California explain that the First People went to the sky when their work on Earth was done, taking their families with them and becoming star people. The Navajo think of stars as "friendly beings" because they lighten the night sky and also because the stars help them tell time and mark the seasons.

According to Pawnee creation stories, their tribe is descended from the Morning Star. The Pawnee settled on the banks of the Loup, Platte, and Republican Rivers in Nebraska. In their tales Morning Star overcame the others and directed them to stand in their appointed places. Morning Star wed Evening Star, and their daughter traveled to Earth, where she married the child of the Sun and the Moon. From this union came the Pawnee people.

In the Southwest the Sun has special significance. The Zuni welcome the Sun each day as "father," sprinkling a little cornmeal and offering a prayer to this great power that awakens the Earth's fertility. And in California the Chumash hold the Sun to be the greatest supernatural being, the one who carries the torch that lights the world. He is both loved and feared, because although he brings light and heat, he also brings death.

ANIMAL SPIRITS

In their mythic histories many tribes recall a time when there was no distinction between animals and humans. All spoke the same language and each received special powers from the creator who made them. Humans, indeed, are often portrayed as the weakest and least able of all the beings in creation. Animals such as bears and badgers, deer and mice, are seen as having distinct spirits and as being "people" of another order.

Many spirit beings, such as Raven of the Tlingit and Buffalo Calf Woman who brought the Lakota their seven sacred rites, have the ability to change from animal to human and back again. Animal spirits may convey the traits attributed to that animal,

An American bison, which came to be called the buffalo by European settlers, grazing on the plains. Among the Plains tribes the buffalo was considered a special messenger from the Great Spirit. Throughout Native American culture animals had distinct spirits, and hunters traditionally prayed to the animals they killed in thanks for giving their lives to the tribe.

such as speed or courage. Birds, especially the eagle, are respected for their freedom in flight. The oral traditions of many tribes portray birds as special beings with the power to carry messages to the sky and back to Earth. For this reason the feathers of the eagle are a mark of special power and esteem.

Native hunters traditionally prayed to the spirit of the game they killed for food, thanking the deer, the buffalo, or the salmon for giving up its life so that people might eat and remain alive. People understood that only with the help of the spirit world could they succeed in life. Someone who neglected to respect the life of the deer he had taken might find that the other deer spirits rose up against him and hindered future hunts. In Cherokee tradition certain illnesses, such as rheumatism, came to the hunter who ignored his duty to honor the animals he hunted.

PLANT SPIRITS

Plants also have spirit, which can be seen in the way they respond to their environment. Plants that are not cared for or treated with respect do not survive. If they are overharvested they will not return. They draw their spirit from the earth, as do other living things. Native Americans saw plants as friendly to humans. To Native peoples there were few if any plants that could not be used as food, as medicine, in making shelter or useful objects, or in rituals. Many different tribes viewed certain food plants, particularly maize (Indian corn), beans, and squash or pumpkin, as gifts of divine origin, provided for their use by the Great Spirit. These traditional foods, grown and eaten by the many agricultural tribes that lived on a largely vegetarian diet, provided balanced nutrition that kept people healthy and strong.

Native people lived particularly close to the land and had a deep understanding of its value. Everything was not sacred, but almost anything, particularly if it was used to help sustain life, might be sacred, and its spirit had to be respected. People had to act in ways that would keep the world in balance and harmony. Overusing a plant or killing too much game could result in total loss. However recognizing the spiritual dimension of all things kept Native hunters and gatherers constantly aware of their responsibility to save and preserve them even as they used them to preserve their own lives.

SACRED TOBACCO

Native Americans considered tobacco a sacred plant and used it in rituals as a way of communicating with the spirit world. They grew and cured a special, strong tobacco. Its scented smoke, rising to the skies, carried human prayers to the spirits. Among the Crow just planting and growing tobacco brought good fortune, and they performed rituals for its planting and harvest. Tobacco was widely grown, and tribes that did not grow it traded for it with other tribes. Present-day rituals still make use of tobacco.

As part of a ceremony holy men and tribal leaders smoked tobacco in a pipe or rolled into a cigar, or they sprinkled it on an open fire. They also placed dried tobacco leaves on water or on the ground as an offering. Many tribes had tales concerning its sacredness, in which it was described as a special gift from the spirit world.

THE SPIRIT IN PLACES

Places were particularly endowed with spiritual significance. Mountain spirits, water spirits, lake spirits, rock spirits—all interacted to make a particular area sacred. Within their tribal boundaries groups had areas—high mountains, bluffs, dense woods, springs, lakes, and waterfalls—that had special spiritual power, much as a great cathedral or a temple might have for a Christian or a Buddhist. People went to these places to seek communion with the Great Spirit, to conduct ceremonies and rituals, and to be healed. In the Navajo tradition, for example, there are four kinds of sacred land:

- Lands mentioned in sacred stories.
- Lands where supernatural events occurred.
- Lands where healing plants, minerals, or waters can be found.
- Lands where people can communicate with spirits.

Land might become sacred when people experienced visions there or, in some cultures, when tribe members were buried on it. Creation stories and other parts of the oral tradition were often tied to specific places, giving the tribe's ancestral grounds special spiritual meaning.

INTERACTION WITH THE SPIRIT WORLD

In Native American belief people interact continually with spirits, both seen and unseen, as they interact with the natural world. The spirit world speaks to those who are attuned to it. The spirits require respect and attention. If no one speaks to them they may

MEDICINE WHEELS

The ancestors of the Plains Indians left behind hundreds of stone circles, often laid out like the spokes of a wheel around a central cairn, or pile of rocks, and with other cairns placed at intervals around them. Archaeologists now believe that these medicine wheels, as they are called, helped Native Americans follow the progress of the year by charting the movement of the Sun and stars. Medicine wheels are associated with spirit forces, and the land on which they lie is sacred. Sacrifices and sacred items were often left within them.

A medicine wheel in Sedona, Arizona.

in turn refuse to speak. Spirits may desert a place that is abused or neglected or allowed to become polluted. Those who have the gift of understanding the spirit world see the loss of spirit in the disappearance of plant and animal life or in drought, and misfortune. If the spirit world is not respected the Earth might die, and all that is on it will die as well. People therefore have a responsibility to maintain life on Earth by praying continually to its spirits and by walking in the sacred way, in harmony with nature.

SACRED OBJECTS

Most Native tribes have traditional objects used in rituals and ceremonies. For almost all groups of Native Americans, these include the medicine bundle, a collection of objects with sacred significance and spirit power wrapped in an animal skin or in cloth. A medicine bundle might belong to an individual or a family, or it might be the sacred object of a tribe or clan.

A medicine bundle containing the wing of a bird. The medicine bundle is a collection of sacred objects that has strong spirit power and is treated with great respect. The contents vary according to the ritual being performed and its link to the story being told in the ceremony.

Medicine bundles are considered to be alive and are treated with great respect. To be entrusted with the care of a medicine bundle is both a great honor and a grave responsibility. Proper care of the medicine bundle may carry with it the power to cure, assure good hunting, or give the caretaker the ability to foresee the future. Mistreating or failing to respect the bundle with its sacred objects can bring disaster.

Among the Navajo the contents of the medicine bundle depend on what ritual a singer, or spiritual leader, performs. All the items are in some way connected to the particular part of the creation story that will be sung in the ceremony. They might include natural items such as shells, stones, crystals, and feathers; sacred representations of spirit gods such as carvings; and other tools of the singer's calling.

SACRED PIPES AND PRAYER STICKS

Most Native tribes have objects of spiritual significance used in rituals and ceremonies. In addition to the medicine bundle, many Native tribes have sacred pipes or prayer sticks. The Lakota people have a sacred pipe, a gift to the Lakota people from Buffalo Calf Woman, the spirit messenger of the Buffalo People. In the Southwest the Pueblo peoples prepare *paho,* sacred prayer sticks that are carved and decorated with stones, shells, and especially feathers, which help to convey the breath of the prayer to the spirits. After making the prayer sticks, people place them where spirits are likely to find them and honor the prayers they carry. They are usually used as petitions for rain or good health and, by the Zuni, after a family death.

MASKS AND SACRED DANCES

Masks are considered to have spirit life within them; masks worn in sacred dances are believed to have the power to transform the dancer into the being portrayed by the mask. Masks are cared for with respect and honored with regular feasts.

Cultures for whom masks have special sacred meaning include the Huron of the Northeast, the tribes of the Northwest Coast, and the Hopi of the Southwest, whose colorful kachinas, fanciful carved figures that incorporate symbols of the Earth and sky, the atmosphere, and the plant and animal kingdoms, represent the spirit world.

SHAMANS

All Native American groups traditionally have spiritual leaders, members of the community who have special connec-

A Native American performing a ritual dance. Dance dramas reenact a tribe's creation beliefs or represent the actions of powerful spirits. Masks are often worn in these dances and transform the dancer into the spirit contained in the mask.

tions to the spirit world. These people are often called shamans, or medicine people. The word *shaman* comes from a similar word used by Siberian tribes to describe their holy people. *Shaman* is now widely used to describe the spiritual leaders of Native American groups, but the names used by the shamans themselves are more descriptive: dream doctor; dreamer; singer; clairvoyant, or one able to see the future clearly; shadow man; head full of songs. The Penobscot call their shaman "drum-sound man" because of the drumming he does as part of the ritual to call helping spirits.

PROPHETS AND HEALERS

Shamans might be called on to cure illness, to find lost objects, to influence the weather, or to predict the likely outcome of a course

The term *medicine man* (or *medicine woman*), used to describe a shaman, is a European label. French explorers described native healers with the French word *médecin,* meaning "doctor." Native peoples later extended the meaning of *medicine* to mean "spiritual power," because according to their understanding, the individuals the French called medicine men were those who were in touch with the higher powers of the universe and could bring them to bear on a problem.

of action. Therefore a shaman develops many skills and abilities, such as seeing into the future, interpreting dreams, story-telling and acting as tribal historian, finding lost objects, knowing the uses of herbs and plants, and diagnosing ailments. Shamans often specialize in different aspects of spiritual life. Some are primarily prophets, seers, or visionaries who foresee the future. Others are healers. Others may be holy men who perform public ceremonies or lead rituals for the tribe as a whole.

BECOMING A SHAMAN

People may become shamans in a variety of ways, depending on their culture. In some tribes shamans are those people who are visited spontaneously by spirits, often from childhood or during an episode of illness. In other groups shamanistic secrets are inherited, passed down to those family members who are willing and able to take on the vocation. And finally, people who wish to become shamans and feel they have the necessary gifts may undertake study with other shamans. Apache shamans, for example, reach their position mainly through study. They must master a great deal of information that is passed down orally and learn to conduct the sacred ceremonies of their tribe, a process that includes receiving details of how to perform rituals through dreams and visions.

Even if becoming a shaman is a matter of choice, there is an element of "calling." If the spirits do not speak to an individual, he or she cannot become a shaman. The ability to receive visions, either to fore-tell the future or to diagnose illnesses, is a

Traveling to the Spirit World

In some cultures, particularly in the far north, the shaman or medicine person is one who can enlist the help of the spirits by leaving his body and traveling to the spirit world, which can be a dark and dangerous place. In general spirit power is neutral, but it can be used either for good or for evil, and controlling it is a difficult and exacting task.

necessary part of being a shaman, and the most powerful shamans are those people who are called by spirits to serve their tribe, even sometimes against their will.

FEMALE SHAMANS

As a rule young women cannot be shamans because of the power of their fertility, but in a number of cultures women may become shamans, as opposed to herbalists or healers of common illnesses, when they pass childbearing age. The shamans of several tribes of northern California, such as the Hupa, Shasta, and Chilula, are usually women. Among other Califor-

A white-tailed deer buck. Shamans use spirit helpers, or guardian spirits, who often take the form of an animal, to communicate with the spirit world.

nia tribes both men and women may be shamans. The Lakota of the western plains call a medicine woman *wapiye' win,* or "spirit-calling woman," one who receives information from the spirit world.

SECRETS OF TRIBAL RITUAL

Among the Ojibwa of Canada and the northern United States, many members of the tribe might belong to a medicine society—that is, they are initiated into the most basic secrets of tribal ritual. Such secrets might include using the drum to expel harmful spirits, magical songs and chants, and the powers of herbal medicines, along with ritual patterns and beliefs. Within the society are different levels of mastery; at the top are the shamans, who have mastered the skills and self-discipline necessary to fulfill the position's responsibilities.

GUARDIAN SPIRITS

Shamans use spirit helpers, or guardian spirits, to communicate with the spirit world. Although in some tribes anyone may seek and have a guardian spirit, a shaman commonly has more than one, perhaps six or more, each of which may have different powers. The shaman contacts and draws on the aid of these helpers by falling into a trance. Some shamans are able to reach the trance state spontaneously, at will. Others prepare themselves for contact with the spirit world by fasting, withdrawing to solitude, self-denial, drumming, or such physical exertions as dancing.

VISION QUEST

The tradition of having a personal guardian spirit that connected an individual to the spirit world was widespread among Native Americans in almost every part of North America. In southwestern groups such as the Pueblo, the guardian spirit came to the infant at birth and stayed with him or her throughout life. In cultures where successful hunting was necessary to sustain life, boys or young men often went in search of a guardian spirit to help them as they assumed the responsibilities of adulthood.

A young Native American dancer wearing a feathered headdress and ritual clothing. Guardian spirits of animals were linked to individuals or tribes and the skin, bones, and feathers carried special significance.

To acquire a guardian spirit the spirit-seeker went on a vision quest. Isolation in a sacred place, fasting, and prayer were the basic elements of such a quest. Among the Ojibwa, when a boy reached maturity tribal elders took him to a solitary place where they had made a platform in a pine tree. There the boy waited, fasting, until a vision came to him. If the spirits willed it he received a vision with information about how he might live a worthy life. At that time a guardian spirit might appear to him to guide and protect him.

POWERS OF ANIMALS AND ELEMENTS

A guardian spirit usually took the form of an animal, but in some cases the form might be that of a natural element such as wind or fire. The spirit the boy saw brought him special powers; for example, a turtle spirit might confer long life; an eagle spirit, purity, and fierceness; a butterfly spirit, the ability to escape danger; or a bear spirit, strength. Among the Plains tribes, buffalo spirits were especially powerful; the buffalo, whose flesh gave food, whose bones became tools, and whose hide made clothing and shelter, was considered a special messenger of the Great Spirit.

INSTRUCTING THE SPIRIT-SEEKER

Where it was tradition for individuals, rather than families or the whole tribe, to have a medicine bundle, the spirit might instruct the spirit-seeker in making one. Taboos, the actions that the seeker would need to avoid in order to live a good and healthy life, often came to someone in the vision, along with a sacred song, chant, or dance. New names were often bestowed at that time. Individuals who received guardian spirits could then call on them for help throughout their lives.

In some traditions, particularly in the Plateau region of the Northwest, every boy in the tribe sought a guardian spirit, and men might seek a vision for spiritual guidance throughout their lives. Some groups permitted young girls to go on vision quests as well. Others, as widely scattered as the Algonquin in the Northeast and the Inuit of Alaska and Canada, expected only those who wished to become holy people to acquire guardian spirits, which would help them in healing and other ceremonies.

LIVING WITH THE SPIRIT WORLD

The Native American way has always been to respect and honor the spirits of all natural things. All things on Earth are alive and more or less equal—in fact, people are in many ways the weakest and least well equipped of Earth's creatures, dependent on the bounty of the Earth for their lives. Angering or neglecting the spirits of the animals, plants, and other forms of the living Earth might cause illness for an individual or disaster for the entire community. Listening to the spirits, wherever they may be found, and treating them with respect is therefore an essential part of everyday life.

Traditionally Native Americans pray with gladness to the spirit of the Sun for each new day. They praise the spirits of the Earth for the food they have grown for them. As they go about their work Native Americans pray in thanksgiving for the strength the bodily spirits have granted them. In effect Native Americans celebrate nature in all its dependable rhythms and surprises. "The Native way," says Corbin Harney, a spiritual leader of the Shoshone Nation, "is to pray for everything."

CHAPTER 3

CREATING THE WORLD: THE ORAL TRADITION

On long winter evenings Native Americans often gathered around a fire and told tales of times long ago, when the world was new and humans and animals spoke the same language. Although the stories might have been amusing, storytelling was far more than simple entertainment. It was the principal means by which cultural values and beliefs were passed from one generation to the next. The time between the harvest festival in early fall and the renewal festival of early spring, the coldest and darkest time of the year, was an important period in Native American life. It was the time when all members of the tribe, both young and old, came together to be reminded of their shared past and culture.

Native American religions do not have a sacred book on which people rely for spiritual guidance. Their sacred lore is traditionally passed down orally in stories of how the world was made, how the people came to be, and how they received the customs that

A grandfather tells his grandsons stories about their religious and cultural heritage at Craterville Park, Oklahoma. This land was granted by the U.S. goverment to the Comanche, Kiowa, and Apache tribes by the Medicine Lodge Treaty of 1867.

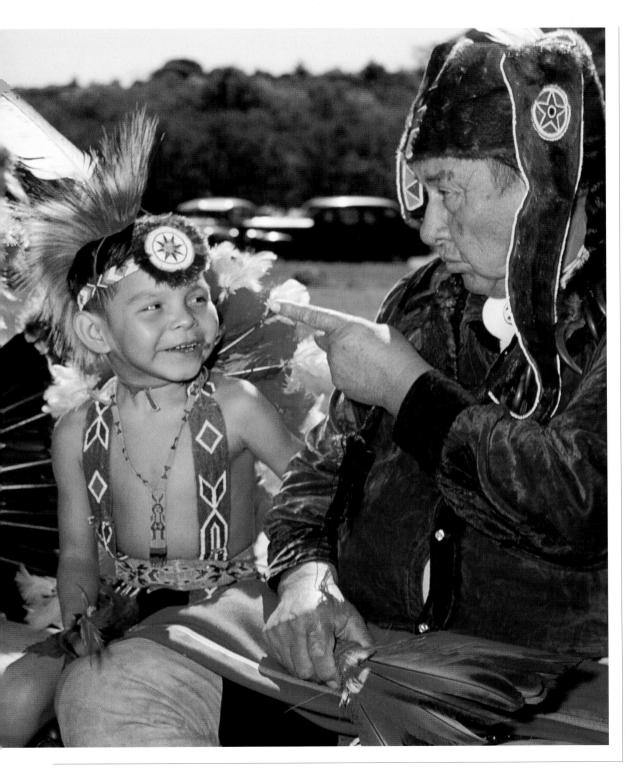

The Spruce Tree House in Mesa Verde National Park, Colorado, is a cliff dwelling constructed between 1211 and 1278 C.E. by the Pueblo people of the Southwest. The dwelling contains around 130 rooms and eight ceremonial chambers built into a natural cave. The stories of the Pueblo people tell how they came to settle the land, and reflect their sacred ties with the animals and features of the landscape.

make up their culture. The tales that make up a tribe's sacred tradition are told and retold throughout a person's lifetime so that each man, woman, and child carries within himself or herself a knowledge of the tribe's culture and belief. Native American stories of creation and the actions of heroes and spirits are sacred to them in much the same way that the Bible is sacred to Christians and Jews; the Quran to Muslims; and the sutras, scriptural narratives that are often regarded as discourses of the Buddha, to Buddhists.

In general the tales in Native American oral tradition are organized in cycles rather than in a linear fashion. Even when the tales are written down they do not form a step-by-step narrative like that in the Judeo-Christian Bible, which is largely an account of the wanderings of the Jewish people and the events connected

with the life of Jesus and the early Christian Church. Instead Native American stories usually cluster around three time periods: early creation, when all beings spoke the same language and could understand each other; the era of the culture hero, a divine being who prepared the world for humankind and taught people their sacred customs; and finally present time, in which people now live and try to follow the will of the spirits.

THE BEGINNINGS OF THE WORLD

Native American tales usually assume that the universe is timeless and that some kind of universe has always existed. Often in those tales the world is covered with water, which must give way to dry land so that humans can live there.

Into this unformed world, either from the heavens above or by emerging from deep within the Earth, powerful supernatural forces, usually in the form of a divine being, come to change the existing universe into the world as we now know it. The supernatural beings who create the world are not the same as the Great Spirit. They are often not even the first beings in the universe. They are culture heroes, beings of divine origins and mythic proportions who came to the people in the distant past to prepare the land for them and teach them the traditions and customs they must follow.

SKY WOMAN OF THE IROQUOIS

In the northeastern woodlands, which extended from what is now Nova Scotia, Canada, to the Great Lakes region, the Iroquois and neighboring tribes traced their origins to a holy being called Sky Woman, who fell through a torn place in the sky. The story of Sky Woman illustrates how a Native American tale weaves together a number of threads that help to explain life and belief.

SACRED LAND

Native American tales often place the tribe in the center of the universe, explaining how they came to be in a particular place. For each tribe this god-given land was sacred. It fed them with crops and game, supplied them with clothes and shelter, and they returned to it after death, becoming part of the cycle of life. Each tribe also had sacred places within its territory, where visions or encounters with the spirit world might occur and where sacred rituals were held.

It tells how the Earth was formed; presents the sacred origins for the foods on which the people relied for their lives and health (squash, beans, and corn); offers a rationale for why good and evil must coexist in the world; and gives an explanation for why people must eventually die.

RESTING ON THE TURTLE'S BACK

According to one version of the tale, the huge sea that covered the world already contained sea birds, turtles, and other water creatures when Sky Woman came tumbling out of the heavens. Two loons flew beneath her and caught her and called the other animals to help. A turtle appeared and took the woman on his broad back. The animals discussed what to do. Finally they decided that the Sky Woman needed Earth. One by one they dived to the bottom of the sea to try to get soil. The beaver failed to come up with anything, and so did the muskrat. Finally the toad came up with a little dirt in his mouth. The woman took the dirt and put it on the turtle's back. The small patch of earth grew and grew and formed the Earth, which still rests on the turtle's back.

SKY WOMAN'S TWINS

After the Earth was formed Sky Woman gave birth to twin sons. They too were supernatural beings whose job it was to prepare the Earth for humans. In giving birth to the second twin, Sky Woman died. She was buried, but her gifts to the Iroquoian people did not end. From her body came the plants that nourish them—the pumpkin (squash) from her head, corn from her body, and beans from her legs.

Sky Woman's twins were the creators of the world as humans know it. The firstborn twin, Tijus-keha, called Master of Life by the Iroquois, was good. He watched over humans, created animals and plants, and gave people customs to follow. The other twin, Tawis-karong, was evil. He made animals that preyed on humans—wolves, bears, and snakes. To irritate humankind, he made giant mosquitoes. He also made a huge toad that drank up all the water on Earth so humans would die of thirst.

THE ZUNI EMERGE

These lines from the Zuni emergence tale tell how the first Zuni Pueblo people passed through different worlds on their journey to Earth. The "precious things" they carried were the fetishes, or small sacred images, that bring rain and crops.

> Our great fathers talked together. Here they arose and moved on. They stooped over and
> came out from the fourth world, carrying their precious things clasped to their breasts.
> They stooped over and came out from moss world, carrying their precious things clasped
> to their breasts.
> They stooped over and came out from mud world, carrying their precious things clasped
> to their breasts.
> They stooped over and came out from wing world, carrying their precious things clasped
> to their breasts.
> They stooped over and came out and saw their Sun Father and inhaled the sacred breath
> of the light of day.

(In John Bierhorst, *In the Trail of the Wind*.)

Terraced mud-built architecture of the Zuni tribe, whose lands
lie in westcentral Mexico and on the Arizona border.

INTO THE LAND OF THE WEST

Tijus-keha could not completely undo his brother's deeds, but he could lessen their effects. He sent the dove and the partridge to find water. The partridge found all of Tawis-karong's monstrous creations waiting to take over the Earth. When the partridge returned and reported what she had seen, Tijus-keha went to his brother's land. He cut open the giant toad and returned water to humans. Then he reduced the size of all his brother's creatures, including the toad and the mosquito, so the harm they could do to humans would be slight.

Sky Woman appeared to Tijus-keha in a dream and told him that he must challenge his brother for the right to rule the world. The two met in a fight to the death. At last Tijus-keha won. However his brother did not die completely. Tawis-karong told Tijus-keha that in the end he would win, for all people would eventually follow him to the West, the land of death.

THE FIRST PEOPLE AND CHANGING WOMAN OF THE NAVAJO

In the oral tradition of Native American peoples stories were not memorized word for word, but told and retold so that their message became part of each speaker and listener. Thus details of creation stories vary widely, not only from area to area and tribe to tribe but even within tribes. A creation story is not a single tale or even a collection of stories. It is more like a tree with many branches spreading out in all directions but eventually going back to the same trunk. The same stories may be told in many different ways, but the basic ideas that underlie the stories remain constant.

"HOLY PEOPLE"

Several southwestern groups tell emergence tales—stories in which the first people on Earth were not created but emerged from the last of a series of underworlds. The Navajo tell how First Man and First Woman and other Diyin Diné, or "Holy People," had to come up through a succession of underworlds where other beings lived. In the lower worlds, the people fought and behaved badly, causing disorder and confusion. The strife brought on by their bad actions destroyed the world, and they had to move on.

THE FOUR SACRED MOUNTAINS

As they traveled from world to world, the Diné realized that they needed to learn to live in harmony and order. Finally they emerged onto the last layer of the Earth, which was formless and covered with water. Talking God spoke to them and told them how to drain the water and make dry land.

Talking God told First Man how to build a shelter. On its floor First Man laid the contents of the medicine bundle that he had carried with him through the layers of the underworld. The pattern the sacred objects made on the ground showed what the features of the world would be.

Then First Man and First Woman created the world. They fashioned the four sacred mountains of the Navajo universe. They put Blanca Peak in the east, fastened it with a bolt of white lightning, and laid a blanket of daylight over it. In the south they placed Mount Taylor, wrapped in the blue of the sky. In the west they spread out the San Francisco Peaks, splashed with the yellow of the Sun. And in the north they put Hesperus Peak, cloaked in darkness. The Navajo associate each cardinal direction, or compass point, with its own special color and power.

FIRST MAN FINDS CHANGING WOMAN

Although their culture developed thousands of miles from the lands of the Iroquoians, the Navajo tell stories with similar elements. A central figure in their tales is Changing Woman, who, like Sky Woman, is responsible for the gift of corn and who bears twin sons. Like Sky Woman, she also has divine origins.

After he and First Woman created the world, First Man went walking in the mountains. On a black and stormy night he heard a baby cry. He went to the sound of the crying and found a baby lying in a cradle of rainbows, its head to the west and its feet to the east. It was wrapped in four blankets, blue, black, white, and yellow, held in place by a sunbeam. First Man gathered up the baby and took it home to First Woman. There they removed the blankets and saw that the baby was a girl.

Each day that passed was like a year. In four days the girl was grown. Her parents named her White Shell Woman, but she is usually called Changing Woman.

Changing Woman gave birth to twins whose father was the Sun. The twins, Monster Slayer and Born for Water, grew quickly and left to be with their father. He gave them special knowledge

EARTH STARTER OF THE MAIDU

The culture hero of the Maidu Indians of the California coast is Earth Starter, who came down from the sky on a rope of feathers to a dark world covered with water. There he found Turtle and a companion, Pehe-ipe, floating on a raft. Earth Starter sent Turtle to the bottom of the waters to get earth. The distance was so great that Turtle did not return for six years. When he did most of the earth he had scooped up had washed away. Only a little was left under his claws. However Earth Starter scraped it out and made a tiny ball. He put it on the raft and soon it grew to be the world.

As yet there was no light in the world. Earth Starter told Turtle and Pehe-ipe to look to the east, and the Sun appeared in the form of a beautiful young woman. Earth Starter beckoned to her to come toward them, and she did, only to vanish in the west. The darkness seemed even greater, and Turtle and Pehe-ipe were frightened, so Earth Starter put the stars in the sky. Knowing that the Sun would return, he created the oak so that creatures could sit in the shade. The coyote and the rattlesnake came up from underground, and Earth Starter called birds to come down from the sky. He made other animals and he made plants. Then he made the first people—Kuksu, the first man, and Morning-Star Woman. Their children filled the world.

One day Earth Starter took the first man to a lake. He was very old, and he tumbled in and was swallowed up by the water. At last he emerged, young again. Earth Starter explained that this was how it would be with people. They would forever grow old and go down, then rise up anew. Earth Starter returned to the sky, leaving people on Earth.

and powerful weapons with which they destroyed the dangerous monsters that had been threatening the Holy People.

Changing Woman used the medicine bundle that she received from First Man to create maize, the corn that is the staple of the Navajo diet. Finally she made Earth People from flakes of her own skin and set them on the Earth, and so the Navajo came to be.

The Navajo trace many of their customs and ceremonies to the sacred story of the creation of the world. The lives of Changing Woman and her sons became models for their own lives. Navajo healing rituals seek to return the sick person to the state of harmony and balance that existed when the world was new.

TRICKSTER TALES

Nearly every Native American story cycle has tales centered on a character we call a trickster. The trickster is a supernatural being, often the brother or sister of a culture hero, who plays practical jokes on people, undoing the good works of the culture hero or otherwise making trouble. In the Iroquoian story of Sky Woman, the second twin is the trickster. Tricksters account for many of the ills and petty annoyances humans experience. Because tricksters also have supernatural origins, humans must put up with their pranks.

Some tricksters, such as the Iroquoian twin Tawis-karong, the Old Man of the Crow and the Blackfoot, or the Winnebago trickster Wakdjunkga, were more or less human in form. Many other tricksters were animals with human characteristics: the Shoshone and other western tribes had Coyote; the Lakota had Inktomi, or "spider"; the Ojibwa, Hare; the Seminole, Rabbit; the Luiseño, Frog Woman. Whether human or animal, they have special powers that can be used for either good or harm, but they also have great shortcomings. They behave in bawdy, irresponsible, selfish ways, breaking taboos and defying accepted standards. They often end up suffering for their actions, but they always survive to trick again. A trickster is often the target of general humor and jokes—someone to laugh at. Not infrequently his tricks backfire and unintentional good comes out of his troublemaking.

Trickster tales are frequently funny, but on a deeper level they point up human failings, such as greed and foolishness. They teach moral lessons, showing what happens when envy, lust, or other desires or cravings get out of control. Some trickster tales hold out hope of redemption as well. And sometimes tricksters, like their foolish, greedy human counterparts, learn from their behavior and become heroes.

RAVEN OF THE NORTHWEST COAST

Raven of the Northwest Coast peoples is culture hero and trickster rolled into one. Raven is a huge black bird who can push up his beak and shrug off his wings to take on human form at will. He is revered for his creative powers and for his basic kindness to humans, whom he watches over and helps.

Some tales credit Raven with creating the Earth by dropping pebbles into the sea. In any case he was the first being on it, responsible for the coming of human life. The Haida, a people of the Northwest Coast, tell how Raven was walking alone on the shore when he found a clamshell. Inside were tiny people. Raven coaxed them out and they became the ancestors of the Haida tribe.

THE PEA POD AND THE CLAY FIGURE

According to an Inuit tale the first man emerged from a pea pod on a vine that Raven had planted after he made the Earth. Surveying his world, Raven saw the man and swooped down. The man pushed back Raven's beak, and beneath it he saw Raven's human face. Raven could see that man was lonely. So he made another fig-

COYOTE

Probably the best-known trickster is Coyote, a half-animal, half-human being who appears in the tales of many Native cultures. In the Plateau region of the Northwest, he is both trickster and creator. According to the tales of the people there, it is through Coyote's trickery that the salmon, on which they depend for food, travel upstream each year. The Shoshone and Paiute of the Great Basin tell tales in which Coyote is the father of the first people. The Navajo say that Coyote caused the flood that covered the Earth before the people emerged from the underworld.

Coyote's tricks sometimes brought him grief. California Indians tell that when Coyote felt there were too many people, he decided that there should be death, only to have his own son be one of the first to die. Coyote tried to take back his decree, but it was too late. To console himself Coyote established rites for people to use when their loved ones die.

ure from the clay of the stream and breathed life into it. It was the first woman. Together the man and the woman had many children, who lived and grew and peopled the Earth.

FLYING OFF WITH THE SUN

When Raven plays tricks he may do it on behalf of humans for whom he feels special affection. It was Raven who brought light to the world when the Sun was locked away from people by a powerful chief. By employing his magic Raven turned himself into a tiny particle in the drinking water of the chief's daughter and was later born to her as a human baby. When he cried for the box that held the Sun, the chief gave it to him to hold. Instantly he turned back into Raven and flew off, carrying the Sun back to light the world.

Raven's trickery often led to the creation of some geographical or natural feature. Thus almost everything people see in nature serves as a reminder of Raven and the creation of the world. As with other tricksters, the mistakes Raven made as he went about trying to satisfy his desires became object lessons in what to avoid.

HOW THINGS CAME TO BE

Native American tales often explained the formation of geographical features as supernatural events, frequently as a divine

A totem pole in Stanley Park, Vancouver, Canada. Totem poles represent beliefs, spirits, relationships, and histories associated with families in a tribe.

response to the actions of people. In whatever direction Native Americans gazed, whether on the Earth or in the sky, what they saw there was related to their sacred history. The world around them was thus a continual reminder of the sacredness beside and within which they lived.

BRINGING AUTUMN RAINS

The Nisqually of the Pacific Northwest tell how, when the world was young, the Creator gave the people everything they might need. Even so, two brothers quarreled over land. The Creator took them aside and gave them each a bow and a single arrow. Each shot his arrow and where it landed, that land became his. The brothers went their separate ways, creating two tribes, the Multnomahs and the Klickitats.

For a long time the tribes lived apart in peace, their lands joined by a stone bridge over the Columbia River, which they crossed freely. However after a while each began to covet the other's land. The Creator, unhappy at this turn of events, punished the people by taking away fire and bringing autumn rains. Soon the people were cold and damp. They begged the Creator to return fire to them, promising to give up their quarrelsome ways.

Mount Adams in the Cascade range, Washington State. The creation stories of the Nisqually people tell how the mountains were formed, including Mount Adams, which is believed to be a Klickitat chief turned into a mountain by the Creator.

LOO-WIT'S FIRE

The only fire left was at the lodge of Loo-Wit, an old woman who was always good and not quarrelsome or envious. The Creator offered to grant Loo-Wit any wish she might have if she would agree to share her fire with the people. Loo-Wit agreed to share her fire with the people in return for becoming young and beautiful again.

Soon the people saw a beautiful maiden tending fire at the stone bridge. The two tribes abandoned their silly quarrels and received fire from her, and for a time they lived peacefully again. But the chief of each tribe saw the beautiful maiden that Loo-Wit had become. Each wanted her for his wife. Fighting broke out again.

THE FIERY VOLCANO

This time the Creator snatched the two chiefs away and turned them into mountains. The chief of the Klickitats, to the north, became Mount Adams; the Chief of the Multnomahs, to the south, became Mount Hood. Even then they did not stop their rumbling and quarreling, tossing rocks back and forth, almost blocking the river between them. Loo-Wit was unhappy to have caused such suffering. The Creator took pity on her and turned her into a mountain as well.

Most of the time Loo-Wit sleeps peacefully. However she is a reminder to people to live in peace with their neighbors and keep their hearts free of envy and greed. If they do not, she might awaken and demonstrate her unhappiness. You see, Loo-Wit did not become an ordinary mountain. Because she had always been good, the Creator let her keep her fire. Loo-Wit is the volcano whose other name is Mount Saint Helens.

WEAKNESSES AND IDEALS

Like many Native American tales the story of Loo-Wit not only explains the existence of the volcano, a mountain of fire, but shows the consequences of quarreling and fighting. Native Americans' sacred tales reflect the high standards of behavior they set for all individuals. People, although they often fall short of the ideal, are expected to live in peace with their neighbors and not be greedy, not steal, break taboos, or ignore the will of the spirits. Bad actions could bring trouble, even disaster, not only to the individual but to the tribe. Goodness, charity, and kindness are necessary to maintain balance and harmony in the world, and the oral tradition made people continually aware of that necessity.

THE SACRED PIPE OF THE LAKOTA

The relationship of people in the here and now to the natural universe is more important in Native American religions than is any sort of historical record. Although tales tell of tribal heroes, the hero was only rarely a historical figure, and usually the focus was not on the hero, but on what the hero did for the tribe—for example, establishing a sacred place or custom, or bringing a sacred object to the tribe.

One of the most sacred of all tribal objects is the sacred pipe of the Lakota. The Lakota, once known as the Teton, the largest and westernmost of the Sioux peoples of the western plains, depended heavily on the buffalo for food, clothing, and shelter, and the animal was sacred to them. They hunted it with respect, trying to take only what was necessary for their lives so there would always be enough. According to legend the sacred pipe was the gift of the Buffalo People, messengers of the Great Spirit, to the humans who depended on them.

THE PIPE OF PEACE

One day a beautiful woman dressed in white buckskin appeared to two Sioux hunters. Although they recognized her as coming from the spirit world, one of the hunters desired her. When he approached her a cloud of mist covered them both. When the mist cleared the woman was as before, but the man whose thoughts about her were impure had been reduced to a skeleton. The woman told the other hunter to go home and tell the chief of their tribe to prepare for her coming by putting up a special ceremonial lodge. The hunter raced home with the tale, and the people built the lodge as the woman had commanded.

SEVEN SACRED RITES OF THE LAKOTA

According to Lakota tradition Buffalo Calf Woman, a spirit messenger from Wakan Tanka, taught the Lakota (Sioux) sacred rites of Canku Luta, the Pipe Religion:

Sweat Lodge Ceremony (Inikagapi). This ceremony prepares the participants for entering and leaving the presence of sacredness.

Vision Quest (Hanbleceya). An individual visits an isolated natural place, fasts, and prays for a vision that will provide spiritual guidance.

Ghost Keeping Ceremony (Wanagi Yuhapi). A ceremony that holds the soul of someone who has died and purifies it so that it may return pure to Wakan Tanka.

Making of Relatives Ceremony (Hunka). This ceremony establishes a binding relationship among members of the tribe.

Girl's Puberty Rite (Isnati Awicalowan). The girl learns her sacred duties and responsibilities as a woman.

Throwing the Ball Ceremony (Tapa Wankayeyapi). People try to catch a ball that symbolizes the universe. Their attempts represent the struggle of humans to give up ignorance.

Early 20th-century portrait of a Lakota man holding a peace pipe and wearing a cross ornament. The sacred pipe symbolizes Earth and all the plants and animals on it.

The next morning the woman appeared. She carried with her a pipe, with the stem in her right hand and the bowl in her left hand. She went into the lodge and took the place of honor. After the chief welcomed her she began to speak. She told the people that under Wakan Tanka all beings were as one family. The Sioux

To the people of the plains the sacred pipe symbolizes the Earth and all plant and animal life on it. The bowl represents the Earth with all its life-giving properties. The stem is the life on Earth, with its energy and strength. When the two parts of the pipe are joined, all of the powers of the Earth come together in it.

In smoking the pipe people are connected to the powers of the universe. Pipe ceremonies were among the most sacred of all rituals, and agreements and pacts made at those times were sacred trusts considered by all parties to be unbreakable and holy. The custom of the pipe is widespread across North America and continues to this day.

were known to be honorable and respectful of the sacred. She came as a representative of the Buffalo People, who sent the pipe. It was to be used as she directed, to make peace between warring nations and to heal the sick.

BUFFALO CALF WOMAN

Buffalo Calf Woman, as she came to be known, spoke to the women of the Sioux, telling them of the special feeling that Wakan Tanka had for them, and to the children, whom she told to lead pure lives and respect the pipe. Finally she told the men that the pipe was to be used only for good. They must always respect the fruits of the Earth. They should help the women in the raising of children and share their sorrows, and be kind to the children. When they needed buffalo meat they should smoke the pipe, and their hunting would be successful. Finally she lit the pipe and offered it to the sky, to the Earth, and to the four winds, from which all good things come.

Her message delivered, the woman asked that the way be cleared for her to leave. As she stepped out of the lodge she turned into a buffalo calf.

THE VARIETY OF THE ORAL TRADITION

Every Native American tribe, large or small, has its own separate, fully developed oral tradition containing dozens or even hundreds of tales. No one knows them all, or even how many there are. Some tales have never been written down or told outside the tribe, because they are considered too special and sacred for any but tribal ears.

Sacred stories tie all of the things in the natural and spirit world to the life of the tribe. Everything has a story—mountains and

rivers; trees and grass; sky and Earth; Sun, Moon, and stars; rainbows and whirlwinds; the foods people eat and the clothes they wear; the deer and the eagle; the rat's tail and the hawk's beak; the infant's cradle board; baskets and blankets; the way homes are built. All of these things are not in themselves sacred, but each has a sacred dimension and all are reminders of the sacredness in life. The oral tradition reinforces this sacredness with each telling and retelling of the tales during a person's lifetime.

Children listening to a traditional Aleut storyteller and environmental activist on Saint Paul Island, the Pribilofs, Alaska. The storyteller uses a drum to accompany his stories of the Aleut people, their history, and their links to the land.

CHAPTER 4

NATIVE AMERICAN CEREMONIES AND RITUALS

Native American religions use dance and drama as a way of communicating with the higher powers of the universe. For Native Americans dance is a kind of prayer in motion, one that involves the entire body.

When speaking of a dance Native Americans are referring to more than just patterns of footsteps and body motions, more than events in which a series of dances is performed. A dance is a religious rite. Sacred dance-dramas reenact the tribe's creation beliefs or represent the actions of powerful spirits. They dramatize the relationship between people, the natural world, and the spirit world. Thus there are dances to bring rain, to make corn grow, for good hunting and well-being, and to renew the earth.

Each tribe has its own characteristic form of dance. In the eastern woodlands people dance as a group, usually in a circle that moves counterclockwise. On the plains the tribes developed

Young Navajo Blue Eagle dancers performing the Basket Dance at the Gallup Intertribal Ceremonials, New Mexico. Each tribe has its own characteristic dances that bring the power of the spirit world to the people.

many styles—circle dances, line dances, solo dances. Tribes of the Southwest use both circle dances and line dances. In the Northwest and among the Inuit solo dances are more common than group dances. Both men and women dance, although usually separately and at different times. Dancers perform not for themselves alone but for the whole tribe. In this way they bring the power of the spirit world to all.

The kind of dance a tribe developed reflected its character and view of the world. Tribes that depended mainly on hunting, for example, had dances that called on the spirits of their game, such as buffalo or deer. Tribes whose livelihood came principally from farming performed rites celebrating the agricultural cycle of growth and harvest. A dance takes place in a special performance area, often one that is selected by ritual means and sanctified for the purpose of the dance. Where weather is reliable the site is usually outdoors, in a field or meadow. On the rainy Northwest Coast the Kwakiutl build special dance houses in which to hold their ceremonies.

The spiritual power of the dance is so strong that according to Native American belief the dancer does not simply perform the role of a spirit but is said to *personate* the spirit, or become a living embodiment of the spirit depicted by a mask or costume. Through that mask or costume the spirit the dancer represents is believed to enter into the body of the dancer, thus linking the human and the supernatural worlds.

PUEBLO CORN DANCE

Costumes representing the spirit world are an important part of Native American dances. For the Pueblo Corn Dance, a ceremony for rain and the health and well-being of the community, a male Pueblo dancer wears a white cotton kilt embroidered with symbols of the clouds and rain and tied with a white, tasseled rain sash. A fox skin, a reminder of the common ancestry of humans and animals, hangs from the belt. A turtle-shell rattle is tied behind the dancer's right knee, and he carries a gourd rattle in his right hand to make the sound of falling rain. On his moccasins is skunk fur to protect him from evil. A sash worn diagonally across his left shoulder is decorated with shells from the Pacific Ocean, the great water. On his head he wears a cluster of parrot feathers to bring rain from the south, and he carries sprigs of evergreen, a symbol of greenery and life.

MASKS AND COSTUMES

In Native American dance the dancers wear elaborate masks and costumes representing the spirit world and charged with sacred significance. Each part of a costume has symbolic meaning. When the Pueblo Indians perform the Corn Dance to bring rain they use objects that carry spirit power and symbolic influence, such as Pacific Ocean shells, associated with powerful water. On the Northwest Coast dancers wear large, stylized wooden masks that depict the raven and other creatures of the area—whales, seals, bears—as well as monsters and other kinds of spirits as they dance out the themes of creation and the opposition of natural forces.

ANIMAL DANCES

Nearly all tribes pay homage to animal spirits with dances that imitate an animal's traits or movements. Hunting dances, which recognized the animals people hunted to survive, were once widely held to honor the animals and to call on the spirits to increase their numbers, as well as to gain the cooperation of the animal spirits so that hunters would be able to take the game they needed.

Totem poles in Stanley Park, Vancouver, Canada. Totem poles are traditionally carved from wood by a family or clan and are a record of the history, relationships, and events that shape their lives.

BUFFALO AND EAGLE POWER

Many costumes depicted animals such as antelope, deer, and even fish. On the plains buffalo dancers honored the animal whose body gave them food, fuel, clothing, and shelter. These dancers wore elaborate costumes that included a buffalo mask and horns, a buffalo-skin robe, and a tail. Buffalo dances were not limited to the plains, however. Among Pueblo peoples the buffalo was believed to have the power to cure illness. After a dance a dancer would touch the sick with the buffalo headdress to effect a cure.

The eagle was sacred to many native peoples because of its strength, its fierceness, and its ability to soar higher than any other bird. In the Southwest the eagle

brought rain. Eagle dances, which incorporate soaring and swooping motions, called on the eagle in its role as messenger to the Great Spirit to carry aloft the prayers of the people.

ANIMALS OF RIVERS AND SEAS

In modern times, with fewer people depending on hunting and game for their livelihood, fewer animal ceremonies occur. In the Northwest, however, people still observe the running of the salmon with traditional rites, and the Inuit still honor the seal, whales, and other animals of the far North with traditional rites. Individual Native American hunters of all areas often observe rites before, during, and after the hunt to ensure successful hunting and win the cooperation of the game. A hunter may offer tobacco, cornmeal, and a prayer feather to newly killed game. The dead game is treated with respect and its bones are disposed of ceremonially.

KACHINAS

Among the most intricate and sacred costumes are the kachina costumes of the Hopi and other tribes of the Southwest. Kachinas are the deified ancestral spirits from whom the Hopi learned their rituals and customs when they first emerged

A carved kachina doll representing the spirit of lightning, one of the Hopi ancestral spirits. The kachina spirits, who watch over the Hopi and communicate with the higher powers, are also represented by the masks of kachina dancers.

from the underworld. Each kachina—and there are hundreds of them—has a specific set of stylized characteristics that readily identify it to watchers.

Kachinas contain many symbols of the natural world. They represent both animal and plant spirits, as well as the spirit beings of the sky and the Sun, the weather, war, monsters, sacred clowns, and many others. Because they represent the spirit world they are not meant to be realistic. A kachina's hair, for example, may be represented by wheat, feathers, or flowers, or it may be cut to indicate falling rain; the face may be a rainbow, an animal's snout, or a pattern of lines and symbols. The kachina also carries or wears special identifying objects, such as the skin of a particular animal, a blanket of a distinctive design, weapons, musical instruments, or plants.

The Hopi believe that a dancer who wears a kachina costume and mask receives the spirit of that kachina. Through the kachina dancer, the prayers of the people are carried more quickly to the higher powers of the universe.

SACRED MUSIC

For Native Americans music has supernatural power. A sacred song can carry prayers to the spirit world, cure illness, and influence weather and events. In the words of the Lakota holy man Red Weasel, "I may pray with my mouth and the prayer will be heard, but if I sing it will be heard sooner by Wakan Tanka." Almost all Native American ceremonies are accompanied by music, especially drumming, "the heartbeat of Mother Earth." Other instruments commonly used in ceremonies are flutes, pipes, and rattles.

MUSICAL SPEECH RHYTHMS

Although Native American music is rhythmic, the rhythm is often irregular, more like a speech rhythm or the rhythm of a bird song than the regular beat of European or Western music. And while some cultures use a musical scale that is similar to that of Western music, other traditions make use of speech tones, with intervals too small to be played on a standard keyboard. These qualities help to give Native American music its unusual and distinctive sound.

The "Singers"

Every Native American tribe has its own musical tradition. To the Navajo songs and music are so sacred that they are reserved for ritual use—particularly in healing ceremonies, which are called "sings." Music is considered too spiritually powerful to be used casually. The Navajo also use song for protection, or "cover," from harmful spirits. When someone is singing, no evil can come within hearing range of the song. The Navajo are only one of many groups who refer to their holy people, or shamans, as "singers."

Vision Quest Songs

In tribes with a tradition of vision quests for guardian spirits, one outcome of the quest is often a personal song. Individual dreamers receive songs in their visions and sing them throughout their lives to call on spirit power for personal success. A song that comes through a vision is considered the singer's personal property and is not sung by others.

CREATING INSTRUMENTS

Musical instruments used in ceremonies are often considered sacred objects because they are used to call on the higher powers of the universe. They are made ritually and cared for with respect. Drums are made by stretching an animal skin over a frame or by hollowing out a section of log. Water drums, which have a distinctive tone, are clay or metal containers partly filled with water and covered with an animal skin. Drums are ordinarily played with a stick or sticks rather than with bare hands. Rattles may be made with hollow objects, such as gourds, hollow sticks, or turtle shells, filled with pebbles, or of objects such as deer hooves or shells strung together. The human voice is also used to accompany rituals in sacred chants and songs or as a kind of background.

SONGS AS PRAYERS

Most traditional songs of Native Americans had a definite purpose, and often the purpose was prayer. If a woman sang as she was grinding corn, the song was probably a prayer for rain or good harvest. A lullaby is not just a soothing tune but words with the power to bring sleep. Other groups have specific songs for hunting or for healing. Many tribes have songs to influence the weather. Most Pueblo songs,

for example, are prayers for rain. Along the Northwest Coast there are songs to quiet storms and rough waters.

Shamans and holy people of all tribes learn songs and chants that enable them to contact the spirit world. Some shamans use the rhythmic sounds of the drum to aid them in falling into a trance. The most sacred songs are never sung except during religious rituals and are heard only by the initiated or by those for whom the ritual is being conducted.

The drum, "the heartbeat of Mother Earth," is an important ceremonial instrument in many Native American traditions. It is considered a sacred object because it can call on spirits and through music and song prayers are carried to the spirit world.

THE SWEAT LODGE CEREMONY

The sweat lodge ceremony, called the *Inikagapi* by the Lakota, is almost universal among North American Indian tribes. It is a form of ritual purification that precedes important ceremonies and dances. It may be part of a ceremony for health and healing. It is both a religious rite and an essential part of the Native American tradition, during which cultural beliefs and practices are handed down to the next generation. A sweat lodge is usually a small structure made of young trees that can be easily bent into a dome shape large enough to hold around seven people.

During a sweat a spiritual leader heats rocks in a fire built outside the lodge and then places them in the hole inside. The

A sweat lodge and tepee on the plains. The framework of the lodge is covered with blankets or animal hides. It sits on the ground, over a hole dug in the center. It is usually big enough to hold six or seven people. Generally there are separate sweat ceremonies for men and women.

rocks themselves are sacred, chosen for their ability to tolerate and hold heat. The leader pours water over the rocks to make steam, a symbol of the breath of life. He or she may also add sacred herbs. To regulate the heat he or she can let in fresh air by lifting the coverings on the lodge. During the ceremony he or she offers songs and prayers for healing the participants or for the health and well-being of the tribe or the world. Animal spirits are believed to come to the sweat, and spirit power is present throughout the ceremony.

WORLD RENEWAL

Most Native American groups celebrate world renewal ceremonies, annual rituals for maintaining order and harmony in the world. World renewal celebrates the creation of the cosmos and the beginning of time. Through ritual and ceremony, people return to their origins, seeking to recapture the purity and power of the newly created world.

World renewal ceremonies differ from tribe to tribe. Tribal groups with hunting and military cultures, such as the Lakota and the Shoshone of the western plains, had world renewal practices that emphasized courage and endurance. People who relied more on farming, such as the Pueblo and the Seminole, centered their rites on fertility and growth. Tribes in California, where earthquakes are common, performed a yearly rite to stabilize the universe.

THE SUN DANCE

As many as 30 different Native American groups of the plains and the prairie celebrate a festival during which they pray and perform sacrifices for the renewal of the world and the people, give thanks for the blessings of the past year, and attempt through prayer and devotion to bring

Opening Prayer of the Teton Sioux Sun Dance

grandfather
a voice I am going to send
hear me
all over the universe
a voice I am going to send
hear me
grandfather
I will live
I have said it

—sung by Red Bird

(In Alan R. Velie, *American Indian Literature, an Anthology*.)

all things into balance and harmony for the year to come. The Shoshone and the Crow call their ceremony the Thirst Lodge; the Arapaho, the Offerings Lodge; and the Cheyenne, the New Life Lodge; but it is best known by its Lakota name, the Dance Gazing at the Sun, or the Sun Dance. The Sun Dance is the most important religious festival celebrated by the Native people of the plains today. It usually takes place in the spring or around the summer solstice, the time when the Sun is highest in the sky, or in midsummer.

THE WORLD TREE

The dance takes place in the center of the encampment, which represents the center of the Earth. A tall pole in the center of the encampment represents the world tree that connects all the powers of heaven, Earth, and the underworld. The pole, from a freshly cut tree, is prepared and decorated ritually.

A lodge is constructed, with the tree as its center. The building of the lodge is a ritual that represents the creation of the world, and while the lodge stands, it is believed to hold within it the power of the newly created universe. The entry faces east, the direction of the rising Sun. The lodge is open to the sky; piles of brush around the outside lend privacy to the dancers.

PURIFICATION AND FASTING

The Sun Dance begins with acts of purification and sacrifice. Young men who are going to take part in the dance are ritually purified in a sweat lodge ceremony and observe a total fast, going without food and water for three or four days. Dancers move for one complete day along the inside edge of the lodge from east to west,

LAKOTA FLESH PIERCING

In the Lakota tradition participants in the Sun Dance, a yearly ritual of renewal and thanksgiving, demonstrated their self-sacrifice with flesh piercing, an ordeal they believed would bring them closer to spiritual revelation. A spiritual leader inserted skewers, or sharpened sticks, under the skin and muscle of the dancer's chest. Long strips of rawhide leather were tied to the skewers and to the central pole, and thus attached, the dancer performed until exhausted. A similar practice pierced the dancer's back and shoulders. Only a few tribes employed piercing; others deliberately rejected it. Kiowa belief, for example, forbade shedding blood during their Sun Dance ceremony. Piercing is rare today, although some Lakota still do it.

An early-20th-century painting on moose hide made by the Shoshone people showing a buffalo hunt. In the center the Shoshone perform the Sun Dance, a ritual of renewal to give thanks for the past and to create harmony in the year to come.

turning around the pole so they are always facing the Sun. They remain within the lodge for the duration of the ceremony, fasting, praying, and dancing. Often they receive a sacred vision in the course of the dance.

CATCHING THE SUN'S FIRST RAYS

The Shoshone Sun Dance ceremony includes rituals conducted at Sunup by a spiritual leader. The men and women dancers move together to a drumbeat, singing a greeting to the rising Sun. They catch the Sun's first rays on eagle feathers that are tied to their wrists, and they touch the feathers to their bodies as a

Navajo Blue Eagle dancers performing the Corn-grinding Dance at the Gallup Intertribal Ceremonials in New Mexico.

sign of purity and power. Sacred songs and prayers complete the rite. On the third day people who are ill come to the lodge to be healed by the spiritual leader. The ceremony concludes at the end of the fourth day, when the leaders bring the dancers water that has been ritually blessed. Gifts and feasting follow.

CORN DANCES

In agricultural areas, people developed rituals and ceremonies to deal with crops and the weather. Native Americans believe that prayer and attention to the spirits can influence the spirit world and therefore nature. Most agricultural tribes performed a ritualistic dance to bring life-giving rain. Other tribes had corn ceremonies and planting rituals.

A ceremony shared by many agricultural peoples is the Green Corn Dance, a major ceremony in which the people give thanks to the Creator and all spirits for the year's bounty. It is usually held when the first corn is ripe. Among the Iroquois of the Northeast the ceremony is held in late August. Among the Oklahoma Seminole and Creek it is held in late June or early July, and among the Shawnee in July or August.

THE GREEN CORN DANCE: SEMINOLE

For the Seminole of Oklahoma the Green Corn Dance, or Stomp Dance, is the most important event of their ritual year. In keeping with the theme of world renewal, it is a time when medicine bundles are refurbished and a new year begins.

In traditional practice all corn from the previous harvest is used up, and a time of renewal and purification is begun. Homes are cleaned and old utensils replaced. The men of the tribe gather to discuss and resolve any disputes of the past year. All crimes except the most serious may be forgiven at this time, and anyone who has been sent away from the tribe as a punishment can return home. During this period the men participate in sweat lodge ceremonies, fast, and drink a herbal drink that causes them to vomit, symbolically ridding them of the old year and purifying their bodies for the beginning of the new one.

THE SQUASH AND TURQUOISE PEOPLE

Among the Pueblo people, who celebrate it in late spring or early summer, the ritual Corn Dance is held to bring life-giving rain. The ceremony combines song, drama, dance, and poetry to pray for rain, harvest, the health and growth of all plant and animal life, and the well-being of the people.

For the Corn Dance, the people of a pueblo are divided into two groups: the Squash, or "winter" people, and the Turquoise, or "summer" people. Dancers wear blue or yellow body paint to indicate their group.

First in the procession come dancers representing the Koshare and the Kurena, the spirit beings who taught the people how to make crops grow. They lead a procession of the chorus, which may number 50 or more. Throughout the ceremony the people of the chorus serve as sacred clowns, mocking the actions of the other dancers and bringing laughter. After the chorus come the Corn Dancers, led by a man carrying a long pole that symbolizes the world tree the people climbed to emerge from the underworld. The pole is decorated with a Sun symbol and a banner, which he waves over them to symbolize rain clouds.

The Squash dancers and the Turquoise dancers alternate throughout the day, performing complicated dances that are the centerpiece of the ceremony. At the end of the day all groups join the chorus for a final display.

"SCRATCHING" RITUAL

There is also a Seminole tradition of "scratching," in which boys and men, and sometimes girls as well, are scratched on the chest, arms, and legs, formerly with owl claws and now with needles. This too is a form of purification. According to Seminole belief badness flows out in the blood from the scratches, and goodness remains within.

The ceremony includes several traditional dances—Stomp, Long, Ribbon, Feather, and Buffalo. The Stomp Dance itself is a sacred ceremony considered to be health-giving and renewing. Dancers who are in good physical condition may dance continuously for two or three hours.

The Green Corn Dance is a time for ball games, and competition may be fierce. The special roles of males and females in the society are recognized, and there are coming-of-age and naming ceremonies for children. Other features of the dance are "going to water," or ritual bathing, and prayer. The ceremony ends with a final ball game and breakfast.

SACRED CLOWNS

People are foolish. They behave in inappropriate and thoughtless ways, out of step, out of place, out of proportion. This aspect of being human is represented in Native American religions by a figure called a sacred clown.

Sacred clowns appear in many Native American ceremonies, particularly in the Southwest. They can be seen alongside processions, two beats behind everyone else, tripping, poking the dancers, making improper gestures at the observers, and generally provoking amusement and outright laughter.

Clowns may be men dressed as women or in costumes with grossly exaggerated body parts. They mimic sacred rituals, only to get them wrong. The Lakota *heyoka,* or clown, rides horseback, but when he jumps on the horse, he is facing backward. Sacred clowns are wise as well as foolish, however. Like other supernatural beings, they have sacred powers. In some traditions, for example, it is the clowns who intercede with the higher spirits to bring rain.

In Native American regions clowns do things that other people are afraid to do. They thumb their noses at propriety to keep people from becoming rigid and self-righteous. They hold up a mirror to human foolishness. People laugh, but they also learn. The clowns dramatize the pitfalls of life's path and remind people that laughter is indeed a sacred and spiritual gift.

THE RITUAL YEAR

Many tribes followed a calendar of ceremonies that celebrated the renewal of the earth. The Shoshone held four festivals, the first in late winter, anticipating the disappearance of snow and the return of life. A second festival came at planting, which also followed ritual. A Sun Dance was performed in summer, and a harvest festival was held in the fall.

The Hopi ritual year begins in November with Wuwuchim, a sacred ceremony that reenacts the people's emergence from the underworld. Leaders ritually close all roads to the village with sacred cornmeal, except the road to the burial ground. All lights and fires are extinguished, and the dead are invited to return. Then a new fire is kindled and distributed to each house.

THE WINTER SOLSTICE

In December the Hopi celebrate the winter solstice, the time when the days begin to lengthen again. Kivas, the sacred ceremonial chambers of the Hopi, are ritually opened so that the kachinas, or spirits, can enter. Men who belong to kachina societies dress in kachina costumes to perform sacred dances. During January there is much traditional dancing. The kachinas visit children and give them presents or, if they have misbehaved, warn them to mend their ways. Older children are initiated into kachina societies and learn the secrets of the kachinas during this time.

THE SUMMER SOLSTICE

Beginning in April, more kachina dances are held. Their purpose is to bring rain, to promote harmony in the universe, and to ensure health, long life, and happiness. Then, just before the summer solstice in June, a 16-day ceremonial series called Niman completes the kachina season. Different ceremonies alternate during Niman. Some years it is the flute ceremony, a reenactment of the emergence story, which also brings rain and good harvest. On alternate years, dancers perform the Snake Dance, which reenacts the legend of a young Hopi who married a woman of the Snake People, and who was able to bring rain to his people during a drought. At the end of the Niman festival, the kachinas return to their homes in the sky to await the coming of the next kachina season.

RITUAL CYCLES

Ritual cycles carry Native Americans through the calendar year with celebrations that link them to the natural world: the unresting path of the Sun, stars, and Moon; the creatures that walk and fly and crawl on the Earth and swim in the sea; the plant life from which come food and healing herbs and shade and materials for building and creating the objects of daily life. Their colorful and stylized rituals, made up of dance, song, prayer, music, sacrifice, and offering, are a recurring reminder of their indebtedness to Mother Earth, the spirit world, and the Great Spirit itself.

RITUAL AND PRAYER IN NATIVE AMERICAN LIFE

Native American ritual and prayer are as richly varied and diverse as the many Native American cultures from which they come. In some cultures prayer is spontaneous, simply "speaking" to a particular spirit or to the Great Spirit. Other cultures, especially in the Southwest, memorize prayers that must be recited exactly in order to reach the spirit world effectively. As with everything else in Native

American religion, there is no single way of praying. However for Native peoples prayer is much more than the spoken word. All life is prayer.

Ritual practices for Native Americans are held in beloved surroundings. Place is important. Sacred places are the homes of the spirits, and they need to be reclaimed if they have been misused or channeled to other purposes. Many areas that are viewed simply as parklands by others are often "gardens of the gods" for Native Americans. This attitude underscores the different spiritual appreciation they have for the same realities.

CHAPTER 5

WHOLENESS AND HEALING

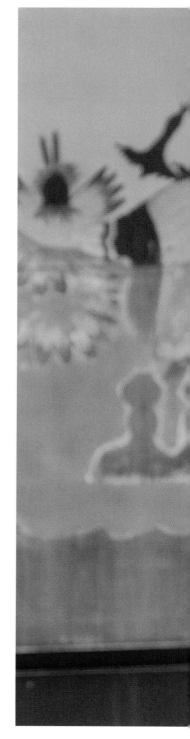

Native American thought places great emphasis on wholeness and wellness. Human health, for both the individual and the group, depends on proper actions and interactions with the spirit world. Well-being comes about through walking in harmony with the forces of nature and the universe. By contrast, illness is a sign of having fallen out of step with those forces. Curing takes place through rituals that restore the sick person to balance and harmony.

Many Native American celebrations have a curing or healing component. World renewal ceremonies, which call on the higher powers to restore the Earth and to bring health and well-being to the tribe as a whole, may also be times of individual healing. The Lakota Sun Dance, for example, includes a time when people who are sick can enter the sacred circle and receive its power for healing. Dancers often dedicate their participation to physical or emotional healing for themselves or someone close to them.

Zuni Pueblo red-tailed hawk dancers performing the Deer Dance, to invoke the protective spirit of the deer, at the Gallup Intertribal Ceremonials, New Mexico.

CAUSES OF ILLNESS

According to traditional beliefs illness comes from supernatural forces. The Cherokee, for example, believe that animal spirits bring illness to hunters who do not pay proper respect to the game they kill. Careless hunting by one person can bring disease to the hunter or to the entire tribe. Other groups believe that bad actions such as ignoring taboos cause internal problems. The Iroquois attribute illnesses to unfulfilled desires and dreams. Among some Inuit tribes illness can be the result of sins committed by ancestors.

People may also become ill because of contact with evil spirits. An evil spirit may come from a spell cast by a witch or a sorcerer—sometimes an evil shaman—or from someone who wishes the sufferer ill. One cause of illness is called object intrusion. An evil spirit sends illness in the form of a foreign object such as a stone or a bone, which enters a person's body. Symptoms of object intrusion include internal pain or injury.

In addition serious illness may be the result of "soul loss," in which evil spirits, especially those of the dead, capture the sick person's soul when it is out of his or her body during sleep. A diagnosis of soul loss denotes critical illness. The patient may have a wasting disease, be delirious, unconscious, or in a coma.

THE ROLE OF THE SHAMAN

Native Americans consider healing a sacred calling. Not all people have the gift to become healers, but those who do must use it or they may themselves become sick by failing to do what the spirits call them to do. Native healers have used healing places and natural means to cure their people for thousands of years. Healing power comes from the natural forces of the Earth, which can be reached through prayer.

Today, with the wide availability of modern medicine, most Native Americans go to doctors when they are sick. They may also consult a shaman, a holy person honored as a medicine man or woman, for a healing ceremony. Native American healing rituals are a form of alternative medicine that a large number of

An Apache dancer wearing a *gan* costume, invoking the mountain spirits. During the dance the spirit of the *gan* comes among the people to heal and to drive away evil spirits. The *gan* are believed to reside in mountain caves.

Native Americans—as well as some non-Native people—use in combination with Western medicine.

In remote areas such as the arctic and subarctic regions, where access to modern medicine may be limited, people still consult shamans and medicine people for many of their medical needs. Although in general people no longer rely entirely on shamans and medicine people for healing, individuals are still called by the spirits to become healers. Most tribes have members who have studied traditional Native American healing practices and conduct healing ceremonies.

INSTRUCTIONS FROM THE SPIRITS

Shamans receive their powers from their ties to the world of the spirits—some through dreams and visions or in a vision quest, others through study. All, however, share the ability to see visions or to enter into a trance to receive instructions from the spirits. In tribes of the North and Northwest the shaman prepares himself by fasting and praying, singing, and drumming until he falls into a trance, a sign that his soul has left his body. The shaman's guardian spirits then speak, telling him what the cause of disease is and if and how it can be cured. Not all illnesses are curable. After diagnosing the cause of the illness the shaman performs the proper ritual for curing it, usually with the help of a spirit. The ritual involves charms, songs, and healing herbs.

Even before the coming of modern medicine, the shaman's ceremonies were usually reserved for serious medical problems that were thought to have spiritual or supernatural causes. Shamans specialized in curing particular illnesses. Someone with an internal ailment would go to a shaman known for curing that kind of problem and consult a different shaman for a sore that would not heal. In addition to serious illnesses, shamans dealt with such injuries as broken bones and snakebite.

An Inuit medicine man and a sick boy photographed in the early-20th century. Medicine men and women received their healing powers from the spirit world through visions, dreams, or study.

HERBALISTS

Traditionally not all native healers were shamans, a role that required not only special spiritual gifts but also many years of study. Someone with a simple ailment, such as an upset stomach or a headache, might consult a herbalist, a specialist in the use of plants as medicine, just as he or she would probably see a family doctor or pick up something at the drugstore today. Herbalists were also considered to have received their gifts from the spirit world, and they often consulted those spirits to decide which herb to prescribe.

Although healers are often called medicine men, many tribes have medicine women as well. In some tribes, the shaman is usually a woman. The Lakota have had many medicine women who showed their calling from an early age. In general, though, women do not become medicine people until the end of their childbearing years, because menstrual blood is deemed to have special powers of its own.

HEALING RITUALS

Different tribes have developed different healing rituals, many of which are so sacred that they are never photographed or recorded. Plains tribes have special sacred objects and talismans that they might use along with incantations to cure illness. The Apache who occupy the mountains and plains of southern Arizona, New Mexico, and Mexico call on the *gan* or mountain spirits for their healing powers and their ability to drive away evil spirits that may bring illness or misfortune. Other native groups rely on animal spirits in other ways. Bear power is considered a powerful healing force by Lakota, Anishinabe (Chippewa), and Pueblo peoples, and their shamans frequently wore bearskins or masks.

If a disease is caused by object intrusion, the object must be located and removed. The healer seeks a vision that shows where the object is and then removes it by sucking, blowing, or rubbing the patient's skin. Sometimes the shaman produces the object that caused the problem—usually a bone, stone, feather, or other small item— for the patient and any observers to see.

ANIMAL FETISHES

Among the Tohono O'odham of Arizona, those who believe that illnesses are caused by improper behavior toward animal spirits treat patients with fetishes—small, carved animal forms. The healer chooses a fetish of the animal that is believed to have healing properties for a particular illness and presses it to the part of the body that is afflicted to draw off harmful influences. The fetish for kidney and stomach problems, for example, is a snake; for rheumatism and foot sores, a horned toad; for children's fevers, a Gila monster (poisonous lizard).

NAVAJO CHANT

Navajo healing ceremonies end with a passage that describes the state of grace and balance to which the participants have returned as a result of the ceremony:

The world before me is restored in beauty
The world behind me is restored in beauty
The world above me is restored in beauty
The world below me is restored in beauty
all things around me are restored in
*   beauty*
It is finished in beauty
It is finished in beauty
It is finished in beauty
It is finished in beauty.

(In Eugene Baatsoslanii Joe, Mark Bahti, and Oscar T. Branson, *Navajo Sandpainting Art.*)

A LAKOTA HEALING CEREMONY

Among the Lakota the power to cure illness is a gift that comes in a personal vision from the Great Spirit. Thus healing ceremonies are highly individual. The ceremony requires objects with spirit power: a sacred pipe; a drum, a rattle, and a whistle for summoning spirits; water that has been blessed; and herbs. The healer sings songs received in a vision, often while touching the afflicted part of the patient's body. Throughout the ceremony the healer calls on the spirits to cure the patient and reinforces the belief that the patient will be cured.

RITUAL PREPARATIONS

A typical healing ritual begins with a sweat lodge ceremony and the cooking of foods for a ritual feast. After the sweat everyone moves indoors, where the room has been emptied of furniture. Typically friends and relatives of the sick person come to participate in the ceremony, because the health of each member of the tribe is important to the whole community. Assistants hang draperies over the windows and doors to make the room dark. Objects of steel and glass and such things as mirrors and pictures are removed or covered. Spirits may appear as light, and reflective surfaces are hostile to them. People also remove their glasses and jewelry.

The healer constructs an altar on a bed of sand that has been laid down for the purpose. The objects on the altar and the sacred fence that surrounds it are assembled according to the instructions of the healer's spirit helpers. Each has its own sacred significance. A sacred fence might be made of as many as 500 tiny bundles of tobacco in squares of colored cloth representing the directions of the four winds, and Mother Earth and Father Sky.

CALLING SPIRIT POWER

The holy person purifies the room with smoke from coals from the sacred fire in the sweat lodge, to which herbs have been added. Then the pipe stem and bowl are joined, bringing spirit power to the altar. The healer fills the pipe and makes offerings to the directions of the four winds. In one variation of the ceremony the healer is bound hand and foot, wrapped in blankets, and laid on the altar. Assistants sing to call the spirits, which observers see as tiny sparks of light and hear as animal or other noises. The patient, and all those assembled in the room as well, pray aloud for the patient's cure and for the well-being of all. The assistants sing curing songs. During this time the spirits untie the holy person and reveal their instructions. The healer may instruct the patient in spiritual matters or life changes or prescribe herbal medicines. The spirits are thanked and they depart.

The assistants light the lights. The pipe is passed from hand to hand, and as it passes, each person repeats the words *Mitakuye' Oyasin*: "All of creation are my relatives." Next water, the source of

A Navajo blanket with an image of a creation myth. Two supernatural "holy people" flank the sacred maize plant which was their gift to mortals. They are enclosed by a rainbow arc.

all life, is passed around. The ceremony ends when the pipe and water have returned to the healer. The altar is taken down. Small food offerings are made to the four winds and then to Mother Earth and Wakan Tanka. Finally the people feast on the foods cooked for the ritual meal.

NAVAJO CHANTWAYS

The Navajo believe that illness and misfortune are caused by loss of balance and harmony, usually as the result of wrong behavior or thought. Health and well-being can be restored by a return to the state of harmony that existed at the beginning of the Navajo world, when holy people walked the Earth. Navajo rituals are conducted to maintain or restore *hozho,* or harmony, to individuals who suffer from illness or who have wandered from the path of beauty and balance.

Navajo rituals are called chantways. Conducted by a Navajo spiritual leader called a *ha'athali,* or singer, with as many as 12 assistants, a chantway lasts from one to nine days. Except for the Blessingway, a general ritual for restoring harmony to the Earth, all chantways are performed for healing. Chantways are complex and a singer may only know one or two of over 50 different chantways designed for various illnesses.

SPECIAL CHANTWAYS

The Navajo rituals known as chantways are a combination of prayers, songs, herbal medicines, and offerings. There are over 50 chantway rituals, each so complex that it takes years for a singer to master even one, and few singers ever learn more than two. Specific chantways are used for specific diseases. The Shootingway is sung for lung and gastrointestinal ailments. The Beadway is a cure for skin diseases. The Windway is sung for many ailments, including eye problems, heart trouble, and even alcoholism. The Earthway is for women's reproductive health. The Nightway cures mental problems.

SANDPAINTINGS

At the center of each chantway is a series of sacred designs called sandpaintings, which the *ha'athali* creates from memory with finely ground colored sand. Navajo ritual sandpaintings are so sacred that they are never photographed, although copies of their designs are sometimes made for study or woven into rugs and blankets.

Sandpaintings depict Navajo holy people, or *yei,* who represent the higher forces of the universe. The ritual calls on the *yei* to restore the sick person to balance and health. The forces of creation that produced the Navajo world are present in the ritual, drawn there by the singer's creation of the sandpainting. The particular paintings that are used emphasize the particular force responsible for the patient's complaint.

THE TRANSFORMING POWER OF THE *YEI*

The singer prepares the floor of the patient's hogan, the simple Navajo dwelling that is also a sacred structure modeled after the homes built by the First People, with a layer of sand. He then cre-

Copies of Navajo sandpaintings displayed for sale at the Gallup Intertribal Ceremonials, New Mexico. Because they are so sacred, the original sandpaintings created for healing rituals are never photographed.

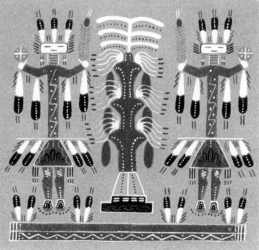

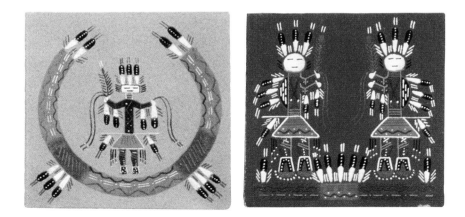

ates the painting by trickling colored sand from his hand to form the images of the *yei* and sprinkles cornmeal on the painting to summon the spirits. The patient, ritually bathed and dried with cornmeal, a sacred substance, is painted with sacred symbols of the spirits.

The patient walks into the sandpainting and sits in its center, facing east, the direction of blessing. Sitting within the sacred universe and surrounded by the spirits, the patient actually becomes a part of the painting. The singer touches parts of the painting and the patient's body, uniting the patient with the painting. In this way the singer transfers the power of the painting to the sick person and enables the healing power of the *yei* to enter the person's body.

REMOVING EVIL, RESTORING HARMONY

The ceremony destroys the painting. The bad influences that caused the illness are taken up by the sand. When the sand is ritually removed, evil influences and imbalance go with it, and the awareness of the beauty and harmony of life that the patient receives from the ritual makes healing possible. In the Navajo tradition relatives and friends come to the ceremony, not just as observers but as participants. They chant and pray for the patient's return to health and may also receive medicines along with the patient, symbolically strengthening the power of the experience and sharing in the cure.

THE GIFT OF HEALING HERBS

Not all illnesses that require doctoring are the result of supernatural intrusion or evil spirits, of course. Common complaints

MEDICINE SOCIETIES

The Algonquin peoples of the Great Lakes region have what is known as a medicine lodge tradition. The lodge, a building in which the rituals are conducted, has sacred power itself. It is constructed to represent the universe, facing east and west, with a pole representing the world tree, around which the universe revolves, in its center. As a rule anyone can join a medicine society to learn its mysteries. Among the Ojibwa, people join the Midewiwin, or Grand Medicine Society, to learn to communicate with plant spirits in order to select the proper herbs to cure disease. People who are ill themselves often join in the hope of finding a cure.

The medicine society has four levels. At the first, most basic level, initiates study healing plants, curing rites, sacred history, and healing powers. They learn the Medicine Dance that puts them in touch with healing forces and strengthens their own life force. To reach the fourth level of the society takes many years of study. Those who master the most difficult healing arts are the full-fledged shamans.

such as fevers, stomachaches, cuts and bruises, muscle strains, and even broken bones have been treated effectively by native healers for centuries. These healers, too, call on the spirit world for help in curing their patients.

Native peoples consider medicinal plants and herbs to be gifts from the spirit world. According to a Cherokee tale animals and people once lived together and spoke the same language. Then people multiplied rapidly and began to hunt animals for food. The angry deer spirits got together and decided that they would bring disease to people who did not respect them and honor their deaths. However the plant spirits took pity on the people and offered themselves for healing.

Cherokee healers can call on more than 400 species of wild plants for medicinal purposes. The black-eyed Susan, for example, has multiple uses: Its root can be brewed into a tea or made into a paste to treat earache, sores, and snakebite. The healer accompanies the use of the herb with songs and chants.

Plants used as medicine are gathered and prepared according to ritual. Lenape, or Delaware, medicine men and women are individuals who have seen visions that give them a special relationship to the plant world. After a Lenape healer sees a patient, he or she prays for guidance, offering a pinch of tobacco to each of the four winds, then goes to find the plant. When it is located, the healer makes a new offering of tobacco, this time by placing it on the stalk of the healing plant to increase the plant's power. The healer never gathers the first plant of a species, but leaves it to show respect and chooses another.

The ritual for preparing the plant includes drying it in the Sun, because the Sun's rays add strength. If water is added to make a tea or drink, the water comes from a stream, because the spirits of running water are stronger than those of a lake or pond. Once the medicine is prepared the healer administers it with prayers.

HEALING THE EARTH

Healing rituals may be held not just for the healing of people, but for the healing of the Earth. Where people have misused the land or polluted air and water, the spirits that give the Earth its life and power die out. Prayers to the Earth help it return to its natural spiritual state. A holy person may call on spirits to return balance and harmony to a place, heal the land, cause the water to cleanse itself, and encourage healthy vegetation to grow.

NATIVE RITUAL AND MODERN MEDICINE

Today Native Americans regularly avail themselves of Western medicine, but they often seek the help of shamans, or holy people, as well, to help them heal by spiritual means. In recent years, as more Native American young people go into the medical professions, Native Americans who have both medical degrees and an understanding of Native practices work successfully to combine the two methods of healing, each of which complements the other. Other doctors may also work alongside Native healers in treating their Native American patients.

Spiritual healing is especially important for peoples who have traditionally believed that sickness results from failing to live in harmony with the spirits or to listen to what the spirits and the Creator tell them. Behavior does not have to be bad or sinful to cause illness; sickness can come about simply by ignoring the spirits' will. Returning to a spiritual place, often on the tribe's ancestral lands, and listening to the spirits is therefore an important step in becoming well again.

Present-day Shoshone healers conduct the sweat lodge ceremonies that have been used for centuries to cure illness as well as for ritual purification. They believe that the heat of the sweat lodge, along with the sacred elements of rock, water, herbs, prayer, and song, rid the body of impurities that cause illness. The sweat lodge cer-

ROCK CREEK CANYON

Where a healing ceremony is held can strengthen its effectiveness. Certain places within each tribe's ancestral lands often have special spiritual power that can be called on for healing. The Shoshone have returned to Rock Creek Canyon in Nevada for centuries because of the healing properties there. Spirit power resides in the entire canyon. One particularly powerful site is Eagle Rock, an outcropping shaped like an eagle's head. After ritual prayer, patients lie on the rock so that the healing power of the eagle can flow into them. The canyon water, too, has healing powers. Sick people who immerse themselves in the waters are believed to leave their illness behind; the flowing water has the power to cleanse itself and become pure again.

emony is considered to be more effective than herbal medicines alone, because of the presence of spirits, particularly animal spirits such as bear, buffalo, or eagle, at the ceremony.

HEALING THROUGH THE MIND

Native healers have assembled a vast knowledge of healing techniques and medicinal plants, but according to traditional belief medicinal herbs are most effective in combination with prayer and ritual. All native healing rituals rely on the influence of the mind on the body, an area that Western medicine has only recently begun to explore. Ceremony and prayer have been used effectively as the major means of healing in native cultures throughout time. As one native healer explains, "A miracle can happen, but in order for it to happen, you are the one who is going to have to allow it—in your mind." In fact Native American medical rituals and practices have been added to the growing list of the forms of natural medicine that are pursued today by many seeking alternatives to the more invasive forms of modern scientific medicine.

CHAPTER 6

THE PATH OF LIFE

I n Native religions life is a path that has no beginning and no end, always leading back to the starting point. In old age people are closer to the Great Spirit than at any time since birth. Each individual may travel the path only once, but for the tribe as a whole life is a continuous cycle of birth, naming, childhood, adolescence, marriage, child rearing, old age, and death. It is the same path that the First People on Earth traveled, and people have followed it since the beginning of time.

The path of life is a spiritual journey, not just a physical one. The ceremonies marking life's passages vary widely from tribe to tribe, but most groups value each stage of life and mark it with ritual and celebration.

NAMING CEREMONIES

Children represent the future, and throughout Native American cultures each new life is greatly prized. Mothers-to-be observe taboos and rituals to guarantee healthy babies. Parents and family members make sure to start newborn children on the sacred

An elder of the Seminole in Florida shows children their destiny on a painted wheel of life.

path so that they will have long and successful lives. Naming ceremonies make a baby a full member of the tribe and welcome it into the larger community.

SEEING THE SUN AT DAWN

Four days after birth a Tewa baby's "cord-cutting mother," the woman who assisted at the birth, carries the baby outside to see the dawn for the first time. She uses a small broom to make sweeping motions around the child, gathering the spirits. Then she holds the child up to each of the six directions—north, south, east, and west, up to the sky and down to the Earth—and offers a prayer to the forces of the universe. Then she speaks the child's name, making him or her a person of the tribe. This ritual starts the child on the *poeh,* the path of life that the first Tewa ancestors walked when they emerged onto the Earth.

The Zuni ritual for a new baby occurs on the eighth day, when women of the father's family wash the baby's head and take him or her outdoors to see the Sun rise in the east. They sprinkle cornmeal in the breeze and pray for the baby's long life and well-being. The Hopi have a similar ritual, which occurs on the baby's 20th day.

THE "POTLATCH" FEAST

In the Northwest the Haida and the Kwakiutl, among others, bestow names at a "potlatch," or ceremonial feast. A potlatch is held by a family to celebrate any major occasion that includes a ceremonial ritual, such as a wedding, coming of age, or funeral. A potlatch includes tribal dancing, tales of a family's sacred history, a feast, and the giving of gifts to the guests. Traditionally the potlatch ceremony was a way of distributing wealth within the community. The more status and wealth a family had, the more it could, and did, give away. Hundreds of people were invited to a potlatch, and each guest received presents such as blankets, towels, kitchen utensils, and other practical items. In modern times the potlatch is usually more modest, but people still dance, feast, and distribute gifts.

SANDPAINTING NAMING

Some tribes hold their naming ceremonies twice a year. Tewa leaders create a sandpainting and an altar and reenact the Tewa creation story. Mothers bring babies who have been born in the previous six months and make offerings of bread and flour. The tribal leaders receive the mothers one at a time and give the baby his or her name. The ceremony makes the child either a summer, or squash, person, or a winter, or turquoise, person—a designation that he or she will keep throughout life and that determines the role he or she will play in Tewa ceremonials.

In Native American tribes girls usually keep their names throughout life, but boys may receive new names as they grow older and take on new responsibilities.

CHILDHOOD RITUALS

Ceremonies for children often mark the roles they will take later in life or the qualities their parents wish them to have. They are aimed at ensuring such qualities as industry, strength, and courage. Tribal elders reinforce these qualities by telling children stories that emphasize them and by instructing children directly to be kind and responsible and to work hard.

FIRST LAUGHTER

The Navajo celebrate a baby's first laugh. Four days after the baby laughs for the first time the baby's family invites family and friends from the larger community to join them for a large meal. The guests bring wishes for the child, traditionally wishing the opposite of what they hope for. They may, for example, wish that the child grow up to be ugly and selfish or sickly and bad

THE POWER OF NAMES

Names have the power to shape an individual's future. Among Native Americans they are carefully chosen, often by an elder of the family or the tribe. Among some tribes there is a belief that the souls of people who have died are reborn into the tribe, and children may receive their names. In other tribes names may signify social rank or designate some characteristic that the namer hopes the child will have.

Girls usually keep their birth name throughout their lives, although among the Mandan parents may hold a feast to rename a girl who is frail or unlucky, and thus give her a new start in life.

Boys may get new names at different times in their lives. A boy first gets a birth name, which he keeps through early childhood. As he matures new responsibilities may be marked by his receiving a new name from tribal elders. Today both boys and girls commonly have both English and Indian names.

tempered. By doing this they are enlisting the spirits of their sacred clowns to help the baby through childhood. The guests all receive small gifts such as coins, cookies, or kitchen items, as a symbol that the child will be generous and kind.

The giveaway ritual makes the child a full member of the tribe. After their first laugh, Navajo babies wear jewelry such as bracelets, necklaces, or buttons as a token of their new status.

LAKOTA RITUALS AND CEREMONIES

The Lakota carry out a ritual in which families commit to bringing up their children according to Lakota values. A medicine woman pierces a girl's ears; a boy may have one ear pierced. The woman threads sinew—a narrow band of animal tissue—or a fine leather cord into each hole so that it cannot close. The sinew symbolizes the traditional way of the Lakota, Canku Luta, the Pipe religion. An elder or a relative speaks to the children about the ceremony and what it means to be Lakota.

Lakota children also take part in the Hunkapi, or "making of relatives" ceremony, where they hear about their sacred history and the words that Buffalo Calf Woman spoke to the children when she appeared to their people. After the ceremony, which may take place either separately or as part of the Sun Dance, families serve a ritual feast and the child receives a new "spirit" name to mark his or her new, more grown-up status. The names are chosen by older relatives from the names of family members who have passed on. A *wihpeya*, or giveaway, completes the event. Customary gifts are towels, kitchen goods, cloth, and other useful household items.

KNOWING THE KACHINA

Between the ages of six and eight Hopi children are believed to be old enough to understand the values underlying their

A Navajo rug being woven on a loom. Traditionally Native American children learn such skills as weaving by watching and imitating their elders.

religion and to begin to participate fully in the religious life of the community. They are taken to the kiva, or sacred dwelling, where for the first time they learn that the kachinas they have seen dancing are not spirits, but tribal members wearing costumes. Tribal elders explain that the costumed dancers personate Hopi deities and the values they represent. The ceremony inducts children into a kachina society and enables them to take part in Hopi rituals and ceremonies.

WATER-POURING RITUAL

The Tewa conduct a water-pouring ritual when a child is about 10 years old. The child takes part in cleaning and preparing the kiva, which represents the place from which the Tewa people emerged according to their creation story. Children choose adults to be their sponsors and to instruct them in Tewa tribal knowledge. The children take gifts to their sponsors and do tasks that signify adulthood—boys chop wood and girls grind corn. The ceremony lasts four nights. On the final night the children see masked dancers perform a Tewa ritual dance. Afterward they have a ritual bath. The ceremony marks their passage to adulthood.

PUBERTY RITES

At one time a girl's first menstrual period was marked by ceremony in almost all Native American tribes, because it signified that she was an adult and ready for marriage. As an adult woman capable of bearing children, she had great creative power, equal to the power of the shaman to heal and give life. Power is by itself neither good nor bad, but it is always potentially dangerous. At puberty a young woman had to learn the restrictions and taboos that went along with her new powers. Women were often isolated from the other members of the tribe during menstruation, forbidden to handle food or to touch other members of the tribe. In that way these young women would not harm anyone accidentally.

Today most tribes no longer celebrate a puberty rite for each girl who becomes a woman. Some tribes celebrate a coming-of-age ceremony once a year for the girls of the tribe who have reached puberty that year. Navajo and Apache still celebrate a girl's first menstrual period with a four-day ceremony and feast.

APACHE PUBERTY RITES

Among the Apache a shaman, who may be either a man or a woman, conducts the puberty ceremony that was handed down to the Apache by White Painted Woman, an important being in the tribe's sacred history. The ceremony includes feasting and dancers wearing costumes of the *gan*, Apache mountain spirits similar to Hopi kachinas and Navajo *yei*. The ceremony is lavish; there may be anywhere from four to 16 dancers, plus one or two sacred clowns.

An Apache Sunrise Dance to mark a girl's puberty rites. The ceremony was handed down to the Apache by a figure from their sacred history called White Painted Woman.

On the first day family members put up a tepee with a framework of four spruce saplings. The young woman and a female attendant, usually the girl's aunt or grandmother, live there during the ceremony. The girl wears a special dress made of buckskin and painted yellow, the color of corn pollen. It symbolizes the costume worn by White Painted Woman. The dress is decorated with Moon, Sun, and star designs, and its fringe represents sunbeams.

From her attendant the young woman learns the many taboos she must observe. Her future depends on how she acts during the four days of the ceremony, which symbolizes the "pollen path," or the path of life that she will walk as an adult woman. If she becomes angry she will be mean in her future life. If she is disobedient she will bring bad weather. She must not smile or laugh, because if she does her face will wrinkle. If she is pleasant and good-natured, however, she will be so all her life, and her life will be long, happy, and healthy.

The shaman conducting the ceremony sings while the young woman dances, for up to six hours at a time, on a buckskin inside the tepee. Between sacred songs her sponsor massages her body to shape and mold it so it will be strong. The young woman may rest between songs, but because puberty gives her special powers, including the power to cure, many sick people may visit her between songs so that she may touch them. At night, *gan* dancers, people wearing the costumes that represent mountain spirits, perform to drive away any evil spirits in the area. They too have the power to cure and may be called on to heal between dances.

As the ceremony draws to a close the shaman sprinkles the young woman's head with cattail pollen, a symbol of fertility and life. He also empties the contents of a small basket onto her head. It contains coins, corn kernels, and candy that represent the gifts that the family will give away. By this act the family's gifts are sanctified. According to Apache belief those who get candy will always have enough to eat, those who receive and plant the corn will have good harvests, and those who get coins will become wealthy.

The young woman dances in place while the guests greet her and ask her to use her power with White Painted Woman to grant their wishes. She then shakes out the buckskin and blankets used in the ceremony to symbolize that she will always have plenty of blankets and food and that her home will always be clean, neat, and tidy.

On the fourth day the guests go home and the tepee is taken down. The family remains together until the ninth day, when the young woman is ritually bathed with suds from the yucca plant. After this ceremony she is considered to be ready for marriage.

NAVAJO PUBERTY RITES

The Navajo observe a similar puberty rite patterned on the rituals first observed by Changing Woman. It is called *kinaalda,* and it is part of the Blessingway, the basic Navajo chant for harmony and balance. The Navajo believe that if the ritual is not observed, the girl may not come to realize the value of womanhood. *Kinaalda* lasts four days, symbolizing the length of time in which Changing Woman grew to womanhood.

The Navajo puberty celebration is a series of endurance tests for the young woman. She runs so that she will be energetic and strong all her life, and she must not fall or look back because to do so will bring bad luck. Between racing and dancing she works, usually at grinding corn. Again her behavior at this time is thought to be an indication of how she will be as an adult. If she does not work hard, for example, she will be lazy all her life. On the final day the ceremony lasts all night, and the young woman must stay awake so that the power that has come to her through the ceremony will not be interrupted, bringing bad luck.

Holy People and the Changing Woman

Rites of passage are often tied to a tribe's sacred history. The Navajo trace the girl's puberty rite to what the Holy People did for Changing Woman when she reached maturity. In the words of one elder, "According to our legend, when Changing Woman had her first period they prepared her by using the dews of various plants. They put that into her body to enable her to produce offspring for the human race. On that account today we believe that when a girl has her first period . . . it is something sacred to us."

(In Peggy V. Beck, *Sacred: Ways of Knowledge, Sources of Life*.)

LAKOTA PUBERTY RITES

Lakota girls traditionally stay with an older relative, an aunt or a grandmother, when they have their first menstrual period. While there they are instructed in the meaning of womanhood and kept busy. The work they do has special meaning. Sewing and beading are symbols of caring for a family, quilting of thrift and hard work, preparing food of hospitality. Their sponsoring relative reminds them to avoid bad or angry thoughts, which might make them nasty or bad tempered for the rest of their lives.

During this time the young woman is taught that all life is sacred. She is reminded to thank Wakan Tanka for the blessings of life and health and to pray in times of trouble or need. Prayers are offered that the young woman will be industrious and pure and will become a good woman, a good worker, and a good mother, one who treats guests with hospitality.

At the end of four days the family traditionally holds a feast for their daughter and invites the entire community. Today this is usually done only for the oldest daughter in a family. Girls' coming of age may also be recognized as part of the Sun Dance or a Hunkapi ceremony, one of the seven sacred rites of the Lakota.

BOYS' COMING OF AGE

Native American groups generally did not have a specific ceremony to mark a boy's transition into manhood. Boys received the privileges of adulthood as they earned them, for example by mastering or demonstrating a skill such as hunting. The family of a boy who demonstrated that he was ready for new responsibilities might honor him with a feast, at which time he might receive a new name. On the plains and in the Plateau regions boys approaching puberty might go on their first vision quest or undergo fasting and other trials symbolic of entering into manhood.

MARRIAGE

Native Americans have traditionally expected young people to marry and have children so that the tribe would continue and

HOPI WEDDING RITUAL

A Hopi couple declare their intention to wed by sprinkling cornmeal at dawn on the eastern edge of their village. To prepare for the wedding ritual the bride-to-be moves in with the groom's family. By doing so she demonstrates her commitment to nurturing her family and her people before the kachinas. At the groom's home she fasts and grinds corn for the family's use. During this time the groom's relatives weave two robes and a sash for the bride. She will wear one robe and the sash at the wedding; the other will be saved for her burial.

On the wedding day the bride dresses in her wedding robe and carries the second robe and several ears of corn wrapped in a reed mat. After prayers at the groom's home she leads a procession to her parents' home. Behind her come the groom's family, carrying food and gifts. When the procession reaches the bride's home and the bride's family welcomes them, the ceremony is complete. In earlier times the couple lived with the bride's family until they built their own house. Now they may simply return home.

prosper. Families often took part in choosing mates for their children of marriageable age. Marriage ceremonies varied, but they usually included the giving of gifts, a feast, and dancing. Today most Native Americans are married in civil or church ceremonies to satisfy U.S. and Canadian laws. Couples may, however, choose to renew their marriage commitment with traditional tribal ceremonies.

MATURITY

Midlife is a time when people become tribal leaders. It takes years to acquire the knowledge necessary to become a shaman or a leader in a medicine society, and it is not until midlife that people master it. Women too become shamans or medicine women at midlife, when their childbearing years are over.

Older people are honored for their wisdom and knowledge. In the Northwest people work hard for material success so that they can share it in a potlatch. Maturity is a time of giving back in a culture that prizes generosity. A long life is a blessing from the Great Spirit. People who attain old age are called on to give advice and pass on tribal lore, culture, and sacred history to children, with whom they have a special relationship.

DEATH

Among most Native American peoples death has always been accepted as a natural and inevitable part of the cycle of life. People expected their bodies to return to Mother Earth and their souls to move on to the next world, where they would live much as they had lived in this life. For this reason the dead of some tribes were buried with weapons, food, clothes, jewelry, and dishes that they might need in the next world. Chief Seattle, a 19th-century leader of the Suquamish people, expressed Native American belief this way: "There is no death. Only a change of worlds."

JOINING THE WORLD OF THE SPIRITS

Funeral and mourning practices vary greatly from tribe to tribe and many tribes compare death to a journey. At Winnebago

Dancing at a Native American festival. Dance plays a powerful role in tribal society and is regarded as a religious rite. It recalls creation beliefs and it can heal, protect from evil sprits, ensure good hunting, and produce fertile crops.

Traveling the Deep Path

The Ojibwa buried their dead in a sitting position, facing west, the direction of the setting Sun and the one in which they will travel. Items they need for the journey are buried with them—such things as moccasins, a blanket, a kettle, and materials to start a fire. Ojibwa dead are believed to travel on a deep path for four nights. They must cross a sinking bridge over rough waters, camp along the way in darkness, and pass through prairies before they come to the land of spirits, a beautiful place of clear lakes and streams, tall forests and grassy plains, where they are greeted with rejoicing and singing.

Wintu Song for the Dead

Many tribes believed that the dead traveled to a place beyond the Milky Way, a land of beautiful flowers, tall forests, and rich pastures. This song expresses Wintu belief:

It is above that you and I shall go;
Along the Milky way you and I shall go;
along the flower trail you and I shall go;
Picking flowers on our way
you and I shall go.

(In Dorothy Demetracopoulou,
Wintu Songs.)

funerals friends and family members address the spirit of the departed person. Usually the speakers explain the path that the spirit must take and they ask that he or she not look back with longing at the lives of the living or linger around them, but move on to the world of spirits.

By tradition the Navajo have always hated and feared death, which they believe happens when the wind of life that entered the body at birth departs. In Navajo belief

A cross marked with feathers on the grave of a Native American Christian. Funeral rites often include symbols from Native American traditional beliefs such as prayer pipes or feathers placed in the coffin.

the good parts of the person's soul become part of the harmony and balance of the universe, but the bad parts remain behind. These evil influences walk the Earth as ghosts and witches and have the power to harm the living.

The Navajo destroy the clothes and possessions of the dead person and are careful never to speak the person's name because to do so might attract his or her wandering ghost.

INTERWEAVING TRADITIONS

Today many Native American groups interweave traditional and Christian ceremonies. After a death they may hold a wake, a gathering of friends and family who sit with the body before burial, in the Christian tradition. However Native American traditions are also observed. People bring food for the funeral feast. Objects with sacred meaning for Native Americans, such as prayer pipes, fetishes, or eagle feathers, may be placed in the casket along with the body. Friends and family sit together and talk about the person who has died. Women may cry and wail as signs of mourning. Music may include both Christian hymns and Native American drumming and song.

After a funeral that is basically Christian mourners may hold a funeral feast. In some traditions, such as Lakota, it was customary to give away all of the dead person's possessions so that the soul would not linger but set off promptly for the next world. A lavish feast and giveaway help to send the soul of the dead person on its way. A memorial feast a year later ends the official mourning period.

THE CYCLE OF LIFE

From birth to death Native Americans live with an awareness of their place in the universe and their relationship to the Great Spirit and the spirit world. There is no part of life that is not valuable. The vast number of rituals that mark the passages from one stage of life to another help keep people on the path, and bind them to their families and their communities.

CHAPTER 7

NATIVE AMERICAN RELIGIONS AND CHRISTIANITY

The European explorers who came to America in the 16th and 17th centuries saw an "empty" land. It had no European-style buildings and cities, so to their way of thinking it was "uninhabited" and ideal for colonization. The countries that claimed territories in the Americas knew that people already lived there, but they viewed these native people as "uncivilized," which to them meant non-European and thus unimportant to them.

Native peoples, for their part, did not understand the European notion that land could be parceled out and owned. To them the land they lived on, like the air they breathed, was a blessing from the Great Spirit. It was a living spirit. Who could own Mother Earth? The idea sounded as foolish as owning the rain or the sunshine. Only after they were driven off their ancestral lands by ever-increasing numbers of immigrants did the idea sink in that the newcomers meant to take the land and keep it.

The Basilica of Mission San Carlos Borromeo del Rio Carmel in Carmel, California. Centuries of missionary effort in the Southwest have produced a blending of Christian and Native American cultures.

A CLASH OF CULTURES

The countries that claimed land in America—England, France, and Spain—were overwhelmingly Christian. They intended to make the new land Christian as well.

A key idea fostered by Western religions, including Christianity, was that their belief system was "true" and other religions were "false." Those people who did not conform to Christian doctrines were "heathens" or "pagans." If they had not been saved for eternity by faith in the one true religion, people either counted for nothing or had to be converted, even if, in extreme circumstances, conversions had to take place by force or by government order.

The explorer Christopher Columbus wrote in his journal that the Native people he met had "as much lovingness as though they would give their hearts." Other explorers also noted that the people they met were extremely friendly—generous and giving, trusting and kind. Many early explorers used Native American guides and sheltered with Native tribes.

In their tradition of hospitality Native Americans at first welcomed and tried to help European settlers, most of whom were poorly equipped for survival in the new land. Many tribes took non-Natives into their families or adopted them as "blood brothers," making them honorary tribal members. Their generosity and trust gave way only gradually.

COLONIZATION BEGINS

The Pilgrim settlers who came to Massachusetts from England in 1609 were seeking religious freedom, but they wanted it for themselves, not for others. They were highly intolerant of any beliefs that differed from theirs. They survived as a colony at least partly because of the help they received from the Native people. The Wampanoags, under the legendary leader Massasoit, gave them seed corn and taught them how to plant it, saving them from starvation. However the acts of Massasoit's people did not stop the New England settlers from thinking of Native Americans as "savages."

As the colonies grew and European culture flourished in America, colonists' attitudes toward the Native Americans hardened. Overall they tended to view the beliefs and ceremonies of Native peoples as heathen superstitions and the people as being ripe for conversion to Christianity. From as early as 1617 the stated goal of white America was to "promote civilization among the savages." Missionaries were encouraged to work actively to convert the Native peoples to Christianity.

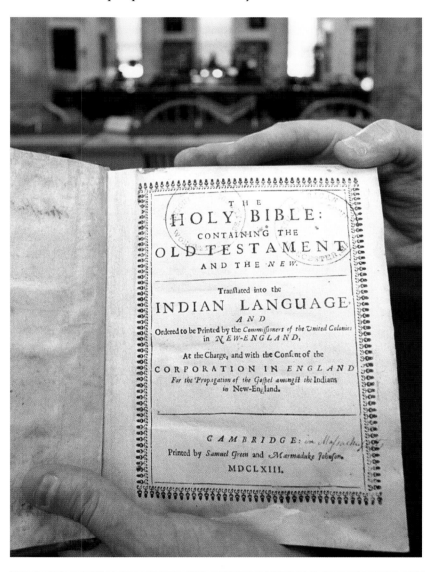

The Indian Bible published in Cambridge, Massachusetts, in 1663. This version of the Bible was printed in the Algonquin language by the English colonists in an effort to convert the local Native Americans to Christianity.

THE MISSIONARY EFFORT

Close on the heels of the explorers and early settlers came Catholic priests to establish missions throughout North America, and members of other religious groups to work among the Native peoples. Their efforts to convert Native peoples succeeded in some places and failed in others. Yet almost everywhere on the continent, Christianity had a significant, long-term effect on the Native religions.

SOUTHWESTERN MISSIONS

As early as 1550 King Charles I of Spain (also known as Charles V of the Holy Roman Empire) called scholars together to discuss and determine how best to Christianize the Indians in the Americas. They reached the conclusion that the Native people were slaves by nature, and they recommended a system called *encomienda,* which gave the colonists the right to force Native people to work for nothing on Spanish lands and to make them pay taxes in the form of crops. Moreover the colonists could use whatever acts of war and violence might be necessary to conquer and convert the native tribes.

Around 1598 Catholic missionaries settled among the Pueblo groups in the Southwest. Over the next 40 years they worked to convert the people. Mainly this meant using Native people as forced labor to build chapels and mission buildings and compelling them under threat of whipping to be baptized, attend Mass, and go to confession. The Spanish actively opposed Native American rituals. They raided the kivas, or religious chambers, of the Pueblo and destroyed ceremonial masks and other sacred objects. Some Native spiritual leaders were hanged as witches. Colonists, including the priests, forced Native people to work for them without compensation under the *encomienda.*

One effect of this Christian attempt to make converts in the Southwest was to drive Native religious practice underground. While outwardly going along with the missionary program, the Pueblo peoples seethed with resentment and anger. They continued to practice their own religion in secret.

POPÉ AND THE PUEBLO REVOLT

In 1675 the Spanish governor of New Mexico, Juan Treviño, arrested 47 Pueblo medicine men and charged them with witchcraft. The Spanish whipped and tortured all and hanged several. Before they could kill the rest a group of armed Pueblo forced the governor to release the remaining prisoners. One prisoner, a spiritual leader named Popé, began to plot to drive the Spanish out. By the summer of 1680 he had enlisted leaders from almost every surrounding village. The revolt began on August 9, 1680, and bloody fighting followed. In the end the Pueblo were able to force the Spanish to withdraw completely.

Popé emerged as the leader of the Pueblo, and on his orders they destroyed the Christian churches and symbols. Christian marriages were declared invalid, and people returned to their traditional religious practices. The rebellion had a long-lasting effect. When Spanish missionaries returned after the death of Popé they did not try to reinstate the *encomienda* or stamp out the Pueblo religions, which still survive today.

THE MISSION OF SAN XAVIER DEL BAC

Some Native groups did adopt Christianity. Spanish missionaries moved into what is now the Sonoran desert area of southern California and Arizona in the late 1600s to work among the tribes who called themselves Tohono O'odham, "People of the Desert" (formerly known as Papago), and Pima. Like the Pueblo, the Tohono O'odham and the Pima tried to resist the forced labor of and conversion by the Spanish. Unlike the Pueblo, however, they lost the fight, in 1751.

In the Pima settlement of Bac, which the Spanish renamed San Xavier del Bac, Franciscans ordered the construction of a spectacular mission church in the Spanish cathedral style. The mission, built almost entirely by Native laborers, was dedicated in 1797. Today it stands on the Papago Indian Reservation created by the U.S. government in 1874. The population of the reservation is and has been overwhelmingly Catholic for more than two centuries.

The San Xavier del Bac Mission, dedicated in 1797, stands today on the Papago Indian Reservation near Tucson, Arizona. The tribes of this area—the Tohono O'odham, and the Pima—tried to resist forced labor and conversion but lost their fight in 1751.

OTHER MISSIONARY EFFORTS

The explorer-priest Jacques Marquette, a French Jesuit, began traveling through the upper Midwest, near the headlands of the Mississippi River, in 1666. Marquette, who established his first mission in 1675, by all accounts treated Native Americans fairly and with love and made many friends among them.

Another noted missionary effort took place in California, where Father Junipero Serra set up nine of the famous 21 missions. He bears witness to the many atrocities against the Native Americans, especially in the protest he sent to Viceroy Bucareli in Mexico City in 1773. Although he has been accused by some of overseeing a system that uprooted tribes and forced Indians to work without pay, he is also credited by historians with introducing many European trades to the indigenous people of California.

THE IROQUOIS

Jesuits (members of a Catholic religious order) moved into eastern Canada in the early 1600s and worked among the Iroquois. They were followed in the next century by Quaker missionaries. (Quakers were members of the Society of Friends, a religious sect that originated in England.) Notably, the Quakers did not try to convert the Iroquois to Christianity. They recognized in traditional Iroquois beliefs the same "inner light" of humanity that they themselves believed in. Certain Christian ideas did become part of the Iroquois belief system, however. For example, the Iroquois began to think of the Great Spirit as "the Creator," a deity with human form who cared about individuals and their welfare.

HANDSOME LAKE'S TEACHINGS

Another factor influencing the Iroquois not to convert to the Quakers' religion and to retain many of their traditional religious beliefs and traditions was a prophet named Handsome Lake (Skaniadariio). The half brother of Cornplanter, a chief of the Seneca, an Iroquois tribe, he had wasted his youth in drunkenness and wild living. In 1799 Handsome Lake had the first of several visions in which a messenger told him to give up his sinful ways and become a spiritual leader of his people.

Although he was influenced by Christian ideas Handsome Lake preached a return to the traditional religion of the Iroquois—really, to his modified vision of the traditional religion, which now included some Christian concepts. He emphasized hard work, sobriety, and family. He encouraged people to accept the benefits of white society while keeping to their own Iroquois values and beliefs. Handsome Lake's "new road" established regular feasts: Midwinter, Strawberry Time, and Green Corn Harvest. The religious tradition he established still continues among the Iroquois today.

CHRISTIANITY AND THE SEMINOLE

White settlement put Native peoples under great social, cultural, and religious pressures. The Seminole, originally members of the Creek tribe of Georgia, moved to Florida in the mid-1700s to get away from spreading European settlement. When white settlers began their move into Florida, the Seminole resisted and so gained a reputation for being troublesome. In the years 1817–18 General Andrew Jackson led his troops against the Seminole in the First Seminole War. At the time Florida was Spanish territory; Jackson's invasions eventually led to Spain's turning over Florida to the United States.

THE TRAIL OF TEARS

Andrew Jackson became president of the United States in 1829, with his reputation as a tough Indian fighter an important part of his image. Under Jackson the Seminole, Cherokee, Creek, Choctaw, and Chickasaw Nations were relocated from their ancestral homes in the Southeast to land in Oklahoma by a forced march known as

LONGHOUSE RELIGION

Skaniadariio, also known as Handsome Lake, founded a new religion for the Iroquois maintaining traditional Native beliefs and combining them with Christian elements. His appeal was so powerful that even after his death, when a new missionary movement tried to convert the Iroquois to Christianity, his "Good Word" (Gaiwiio) endured. Eventually Handsome Lake's teachings evolved into an Iroquois religious movement known as the Longhouse Religion, after the traditional building where meetings are held. This religion is still practiced among the Iroquois.

Osceola, chief of the Seminole people, led the fight against U.S. troops in Florida to maintain the independence of his people in the Second Seminole War of 1835.

the Trail of Tears. Forced to walk the great distance, many thousands of these people died.

Some Seminole fled into the Florida Everglades, where they continued to wage war against U.S. troops. In 1835 the Second Seminole War broke out. Under their leader Osceola, the Seminole fought cleverly and effectively. Even after Osceola had been captured and had died in prison, they continued to fight. The war finally wound down in 1842 without a decisive victory on either side and without surrender by the Seminole. Another effort to control and relocate the Seminole took place from 1855 to 1858 but was also unsuccessful. Descendants of this Seminole band live in Florida to this day.

BLENDING OF RELIGIONS

Baptist missionaries, preaching in the Seminole language, began working to convert the people as they arrived on the Oklahoma reservation. The two religions blended, as Christian traditions worked their way into Seminole rituals and vice versa. Stomp Dance songs took on the character of Christian gospel music, led by a singer who sang each line for people to follow. Christian churches developed hymns in the Seminole language with Native American tunes. Seminole Baptist churches featured fasting and spontaneous prayer and preaching, holdovers from Seminole rites. As people adapted to their new surroundings they identified new places as sacred and would sometimes withdraw to them to seek a vision or the answer to a problem from the Christian God.

WEAKENING TRIBAL BONDS

The Seminole who remained in Florida met Christianity in the early 1900s when converts from their own tribe began to preach to them in their own language. A sizable portion of the tribe converted, rejecting traditional Seminole ritual and belief. The Seminole Christians refused to participate in rituals such as the Green Corn Dance, the world renewal ceremony that had been at the center of Seminole culture. Although traditional practices continued among the people who had not converted, religious differences weakened tribal bonds.

THE RESERVATION SYSTEM

During the 1800s many other tribes were forced onto reservations, often thousands of miles from their ancestral homes. These reservations were frequently located on land no one else wanted. Agricultural tribes found themselves on barren, dry plains where nothing would grow, and hunting tribes found themselves on land where little if any game was available. People were separated from their sacred sites. Reservations became places of unemployment, poverty, and alcoholism, places where people lived in great despair.

Tribes like the Navajo and Hopi, parts of whose ancestral lands were designated as reservations, fared better. Because they remained close to their sacred sites they were able to maintain their traditional culture and religion to a large degree. However, these places too suffered economically.

BANS ON NATIVE RELIGIOUS PRACTICE

By the mid-1800s there were few places left in America that Native Americans could go to escape the spread of white culture. In the 1700s settlement in the East had forced them onto the plains. When the railroad cut through the plains, even that place was no longer a haven.

Contact with white America threw Native American society into cultural and religious conflict. Pressures to conform to modern ways led people away from traditional beliefs and toward acceptance of Christianity. Native Americans began, like the white society around them, to separate the sacred from the secular, something they had never done before.

THE COURTS OF INDIAN OFFENSES

When Native Americans were forced off their ancestral lands and moved onto reservations, they came under government

THE DANCE CONTINUED

Under federal government rulings the Sun Dance became illegal, along with other feasts and dances. The Sun Dance had been central to the cultural and religious life of the Plains tribes. They searched for ways to continue it. They dropped aspects that the white officials objected to and presented it as a cultural festival rather than a religious ceremony. The Shoshone added Christian symbolism. Somewhat changed in character, the dance continued.

control. The U.S. Bureau of Indian Affairs put white appointees, known as Indian agents, in charge of administering tribal business. These agents made regulations that were often enacted into law by the federal government. The Courts of Indian Offenses, established in 1883, banned "old heathenish dances." It also barred medicine men from performing rituals and ordered an end to some mourning practices, such as the destruction of property. Its rulings remained in place until 1934.

Members of the Crow tribe on the Crow Reservation in Montana. During the 19th century many tribes were forced onto reservations with poor farming or hunting, making it almost impossible to survive in their traditional ways.

PEOPLE OF THE NORTHWEST

In Canada from 1876 to 1951 it was illegal for Native Americans to practice their religious rites. On the Northwest Coast Native Americans did manage to conduct some ceremonies in secret; others they changed to make them more acceptable to white authorities. The potlatch ceremony, for example, became more of a secular giveaway than a religious ceremony.

Many Northwest Indians became Christian during this time. The difficulties of maintaining traditional ways led many people to abandon ancestral religions. In the 75 years of the ban some traditions were lost as spiritual leaders died without passing on their knowledge.

JOHN SLOCUM AND THE INDIAN SHAKER CHURCH

In the late 1800s a religious leader, John Slocum, emerged in the Northwest. He was a member of the Squaxin, a Salish people on Puget Sound in Washington State. In 1881, when Slocum was about 40 years old, a logging accident apparently took his life. His body was prepared for burial and the mourners gathered. Suddenly he sat up and began to speak. Slocum told the astonished group that he had indeed died and had gone to the Christian heaven, where he saw a great light. An angel had sent him back with a message: People were to give up the practice of shamanism. They must avoid sins like smoking, gambling, and drinking and must pray regularly.

A SIGN OF GREAT MEDICINE POWER

Slocum's followers built him a church in which he preached a basically Christian message. Slocum was influenced by Catholicism, and he used aspects of Christian symbolism, such as a steeple, a cross, and handbell ringing. However the church had echoes of traditional Native American ritual as well. The preacher muttered words to an interpreter to be spoken aloud to listeners in the way of a shaman. The service was followed by a ceremonial feast in which people sat by their rank in the tribe, as at a potlatch. It was a unique combination of religions.

About a year later Slocum became ill and again appeared to die. His wife, Mary, called for his body to be brought back to their house. She began to tremble violently and to pray aloud to Jesus, and Slocum began to show signs of life. After his recovery he too adopted the custom of trembling or "shaking," believing it to be a sign of the great medicine power promised by the angel he had seen in his earlier vision.

SHAMANIC RITUAL AND HEALING

Slocum's message was attractive to Native people because it came from the direct experience of another Native American. His Indian Shaker Church, as it was named, gained many followers. It spread throughout the Northwest and into California. Local Protestant missionaries opposed it. They had Slocum jailed and forced him to attend Presbyterian services. The opposition ended, however, in 1892, when the Indian Shakers organized legally. The Indian Shaker Church took on many of the roles of the shaman, such as curing and finding lost objects, but members professed belief in God and Jesus, not the spirit world. Although small, the church still survives and still attracts converts, often people who believe they had come to be cured of illness through the power of prayer.

INDIAN SCHOOLS

The U.S. government mandated formal education for Native American young people. Children, always considered the hope and future of a tribe, had always learned their skills and cultural traditions one-on-one from their elders, by watching and being included. Now Christian missionaries were moving onto the reservations and establishing churches and schools. As young people reached school age they were shipped off to boarding schools, often hundreds of miles from their homes, too distant for families to visit. In the summers they were often sent to work for non-Indian families so they would be immersed in the life of the "white man." Schools such as the Chilocco Indian School of Oklahoma, founded in 1884, and the Carlisle Indian School of

Pennsylvania, founded in 1887, taught classes in English, and students were punished for speaking their Native language. The schools banned Native traditions and presented Christian beliefs instead.

By the time the young people graduated and returned to their homes on the reservation, many had lost their language and culture. Taught to believe that their own traditions were backward and superstitious, and resenting the Christian beliefs that had been forced on them, they felt lost in both worlds. Meanwhile the spiritual leaders of an earlier generation were dying out. The young people to whom they should have been passing sacred knowledge no longer spoke their language. It was a bleak time for Native religions.

Tepees set up in front of a large boarding school for Native Americans in Pine Ridge, South Dakota. From a young age until they graduated, Native American children were made to go to boarding schools where they had to speak English and abandon their Native traditions.

THE GHOST DANCE

The Northern Paiute or, in their own language, the Numu, "the People," of the Walker River area in Nevada, suffered enormously through the middle of the 19th century. Miners on their way to the California gold rush (1849) cut through their lands, destroying farmland and killing game. Then homesteaders moved in, taking the best land for themselves. The Numu fought back but federal troops moved in and an uneasy truce began. A long drought brought hunger and the diseases of the white man, to which the Indians had no natural immunity, causing many of them to die.

On New Year's Day 1889 a Northern Paiute named Wovoka had a vision. In it a messenger from God told him to preach that

THE FINAL GHOST DANCE

The Ghost Dance movement that developed among the Numu in the late-19th century spread across tribal lines. Among the Lakota, bitter about the loss of their lands to white interests, years of bloody warfare with federal troops, and a string of broken governmental promises, the Ghost Dance evolved to fit their needs. It became more warlike.

One feature of the dance among the Lakota was the Ghost Shirt, a buckskin garment decorated with symbols that was believed to protect the wearer from bullets. At the tragic massacre at Wounded Knee a Lakota leader prayed that the Ghost Shirt would protect them, but more than 150 Lakota were shot and killed by soldiers.

Late 19th-century photograph of the Lakota Sioux performing a Ghost Dance.

Indians and white people must be at peace. He also received special powers, including the gift of predicting weather and making rain, and was told to introduce the Ghost Dance, a round dance for spiritual renewal, in which people held hands and moved in a circle singing holy songs. During the dance people often saw visions of dead relatives returning.

WODZIWOB'S PROPHECY

Wovoka was a shaman's son and had probably learned shamanistic skills from his father. As a child, he had heard the prophesies of Wodziwob, an earlier Numu prophet who had foreseen a time when the dead Native Americans would arise, the buffalo would return, and white people would be gone. In addition Wovoka had grown up with white companions. At their home he had listened to stories from the Christian Bible. All of these elements combined to make Wovoka one of the great spiritual leaders of Native America.

News of Wovoka's vision spread. The Ghost Dance movement crossed tribal lines and united people who had remained separate for centuries.

THE DEATH OF SITTING BULL AND THE WOUNDED KNEE MASSACRE

U.S. government agents viewed the Ghost Dance with alarm. They placed an absolute ban on its performance. At that time they were repressing all Native rituals, but the Ghost Dance made them particularly nervous. Soldiers believed that it was a war dance meant to whip the dancers into a frenzy for battle. Rumors that a Ghost Dance was going to be held led to an order for the tribal police to arrest Sitting Bull, a Lakota chief and spiritual leader. As he was seized fighting broke out, and he was killed along with 11 others.

Arapaho Ghost Dance Song

The Ghost Dance Religion gave people who had lost almost everything an outlet for their suffering. As they danced they sang, sometimes with joy and other times as an expression of their sorrow.

Father, have pity on me
I am crying for thirst,
all is gone,
I have nothing to eat.

—Anonymous, 1894

(In John Bierhorst, *A Cry from the Earth: Music of the North American Indians.*)

Tribal leaders had never wanted to get into a battle with the United States. Sitting Bull's death frightened them. Another leader, Chief Big Foot, set out to lead his people to the Pine Ridge Reservation in North Dakota, where he felt they would be safe. However before they could get there they were surrounded by U.S. Army troops and forced to camp at Wounded Knee Creek, where the soldiers trained machine guns on them. One of the leaders prayed aloud that the men's Ghost Shirts would protect them. Skirmishes broke out and then the shooting began in earnest. The soldiers killed more than 150 men, women, and children in what came to be known as the Wounded Knee Massacre. Wovoka, in mourning, ordered that the Ghost Dances stop. For the most part the Ghost Dance religion ended, although some small groups continued to practice it into the 20th century.

THE NATIVE AMERICAN CHURCH

The Ghost Dance of 1890 had appealed to Native Americans of many different tribes. For the first time they had begun to think of themselves less as members of individual tribes and more as "Native Americans." Politically, members of different tribes joined together in what was called the pan-Indian movement, which welcomed Native Americans of all tribal backgrounds. In the early-20th century, an organization called the Native American Church was developed by those who practiced the peyote ritual, filling the gap left when the Ghost Dance died out. It blends native beliefs with aspects of Christianity.

THE USE OF PEYOTE

A controversial aspect of the Native American Church has been the use of peyote, the fruit of a southwestern cactus that is a mild hallucinogen, or drug that alters consciousness. It was said that eating a small quantity of peyote might help people to have "visions" or cause them to see colored lights around objects. Native American Church members compare their use of peyote to the use of sacramental wine in Christian communion and give it the same reverance.

Bans on the use of peyote go back to 1620, when the Spanish declared its use to be heresy. By the end of the 19th century Christian missionaries and Indian agents called peyote use a "heathen superstition" that had to be replaced by Christianity. In 1888 the Indian agent of the Kiowa, Comanche, and Wichita tribes banned its use in religious ceremonies. Two years later the ban was adopted by the U.S. government. Government agents raided peyote ceremonies. They arrested worshippers, who were sent to jail or fined, and seized property on which the ceremony was conducted.

Acts of Congress passed in 1965 and 1970 allowed the use of peyote for religious purposes, but arrests continued. Some federal officials still seized peyote even after the American Indian Religious Freedom Act of 1978 specifically permitted its use.

THE PEYOTE RITUAL

There are two versions of the basic peyote ritual: the Half-Moon Ceremony (Tepee Way) and the Quanah Parker, or Kiowa, Way. Both are similar. The peyote ritual takes place around a crescent- or horseshoe-shaped earthen altar. The ritual leader, called the roadman, holds a feathered staff and a rattle. He is assisted by the chief drummer, who beats the water drum; cedarman, who holds a bag of cedar needles; and fireman, who makes and tends the fire, which has four logs pointing in the four directions of the compass. The leader passes the peyote around the circle along with the rattle, and each participant takes some of the peyote and sings.

During the ceremony those taking part may see spirits or angels or may receive instructions on how to live a better life. They call on the peyote spirit, whom they see as one with God, Christ, and the Great

Peyote Woman

Peyote has been a part of Native American ritual for more than 10,000 years. An ancient Kiowa tale tells of a woman who was about to give birth. Traveling with her people across the desert, she fell behind and bore her child alone in the desert. She was ready to give up in despair when the spirit of the peyote came to her and told her to eat some of the plant. The peyote spirit gave her strength and led her home. She taught the people the spirit's prayers and songs and began the peyote tradition, and she is honored as Peyote Woman.

Spirit. The ceremony cleanses the participants of evil influences. At the end a woman who symbolizes Peyote Woman brings water to the participants, and they refresh themselves. Afterward people come to be healed and to testify about how the religion has made them better people. The peyote road, as it is called, demands high moral standards. People must not drink, gamble, or quarrel, must work hard, and must treat their families with love and respect.

AN INDIGENOUS CHURCH

Peyotism filled a need that many Native Americans felt for a religion of their own not dominated by white America. In 1944 it was incorporated as the Native American Church of the United States; five years later it changed its name to the Native American Church of North America to include Canadians. While information is somewhat elusive, recent estimates give the number of fol-

A tepee is seen with Wounded Knee Church in the background, at Wounded Knee in the Pine Ridge Reservation, South Dakota. Wounded Knee is the site of the massacre of some 150 Lakota Sioux men, women and children, by the U.S. Army in 1890.

lowers as 100,000 to 225,000. It is incorporated in 17 states but is still the religion of only a small minority of Native Americans. Some tribes have no adherents.

CHRISTIANITY AND NATIVE RELIGIONS

Contact with Christian European-Americans meant great challenge and change for Native Americans. From the outset many Native American spiritual leaders recognized in the Christian God similarities to the Great Spirit that they had worshipped from the beginning of time. The European settlers who colonized North America, however, for the most part rejected any such relationship. Missionary efforts and government policies directly assaulted Native American religions as European settlement assaulted their culture.

Native Americans met the challenge in different ways. Many embraced Christianity. Others adapted and incorporated aspects of it into their own belief systems. Christian thought influenced a number of religious movements that remain distinctively Native American, including the Iroquois Longhouse Religion, the Indian Shaker Church, the Ghost Dance Religion, and the Native American Church.

In spite of 400 years of strong efforts to stamp out Native American religions, a number of them, particularly in the American Southwest and the plains but in other parts of North America as well, have continued into the present. Their survival demonstrates the strength and vitality of Native American religious belief.

CHAPTER 8

NATIVE AMERICAN RELIGIONS TODAY

For much of the 20th century Native American Indians were often described as the "Vanishing Americans." Their numbers were decreasing and Native American identity was disappearing, as many American Indians were being assimilated into urban American society. This was especially true during World War II (1939–45), when many Native Americans found employment in wartime industries in or near large cities. Ironically many of them lost these same jobs when soldiers returned home. In the 1950s Indians seemed truly to vanish from American and Canadian awareness.

In the 1960s this portrait of the "Vanishing Americans" began to change dramatically. North American Indians in Canada and the United States started to focus on their legal status, which had been established through century-old treaties between Indian nations and the different governments. In October 1969 a fire at the Indian Center in San Francisco, which housed many of the social services for Native Americans, stimulated some of

Navajo tribal legislators and family members ride into Window Rock, Arizona, in 2006 to start the Navajo Nation Council summer session. Since the late-20th century Native Americans have been increasingly aware of the treaties and settlements previously ignored by government authorities, giving them rights as independent nations.

this new approach. The center was burned down the night after urban Native American groups held a convention there. Based on a treaty of 1868 that granted the island of Alcatraz to the Sioux, a group of 200 Native Americans took over Alcatraz and demanded title to the island as a spiritual retreat, a university, and a center for the social services that had been destroyed by the fire. Throughout the year and a half that they occupied the island the Native Americans received a great deal of attention to their cause, especially by calling themselves "Indians of All Tribes."

Other local protests took place in the United States and Canada, such as the protest at the Gallup Ceremonial. Largely controlled by non-Native Americans of Gallup, New Mexico, they gave little support to Native American participants. This protest seriously split the Native American community. The elders, who wanted to guarantee their gains from the Native American pottery sales at the Ceremonial, opposed the younger protesters.

Members of the Western Shoshone tribe look toward the rising Sun during a ceremony near the gates to the Nevada nuclear test site and the proposed Yucca Mountain nuclear waste dump at Mercury, Nevada, in May 2002. Yucca Mountain is sacred to the Shoshone religion, but plans are going ahead to open the site as a final repository for high-level nuclear waste in 2010.

The youthful element captured the imagination of many other younger Native Americans throughout the United States and stimulated the growth of pride in their tribal life and customs. Native pride also grew in Canada. This can be seen in the 1990 standoff between the Mohawk and the Canadian Army over land issues that eventually led to a government study of Canadian policies regarding its Native peoples. A report released in 1996 made more than 400 recommendations for improving the relationship between Canada and its Indians and Inuit. Recommendations included recognition of the Native tribes that live in Canada's 633 reservations as sovereign nations, empowered to govern themselves without undue government interference.

Such local or grassroots protests had national effects, both in the United States and Canada, and captured the interest and support of many non-Indians. Non-Native Americans' interest in Native American culture and religious beliefs and practices grew. This was an era when many different groups were growing in the self-awareness of really belonging to the American—and the Canadian—dream. Indian pride benefited from these diverse forces. Native Americans felt newly confirmed and supported not only by their own people, but by many others as well.

CHANGING TIMES

The period from the 1960s to the 1990s was a time of political change and growth in ethnic consciousness. It was also a time when Native Americans in particular became increasingly aware of the vast legal foundation they had for their causes. Many treaties and settlements that had formally guaranteed Native Americans independence through laws had been ignored; their implementation had been neglected. The legal status of Indian tribes as independent nations within the borders of the United States and Canada was, in effect, more solid legally than the appeals of all minorities—including Native Americans—to human rights. Although the Native Americans did pursue human rights, they also claimed legal rights that officially granted them strength and independence.

DEVELOPING TRADITIONS AND ENSURING RIGHTS

The practical fulfillment of this new awareness would not be easily achieved. It was one thing for Native Americans to challenge publicly the stereotypes that they felt harmed and demeaned them and to gripe against government policies that they found objectionable. It was another thing altogether to fight the legal and personal battles necessary to retain and increase the resources needed to preserve and develop Native cultural and religious traditions that had been forgotten or erased.

Tribal councils in the United States and Canada became more active in negotiating with their governments. Many Indian nations of the United States already had constitutions and political structures parallel to those outlined in the U.S. Constitution. The United States recognized these tribes as separate nations within U.S. boundaries. Native Americans found that they could use these structures to govern themselves and ensure their rights.

LEGACY OF THE PAST AND RECOVERY

The creation of separate nations has, however, also brought problems. For example, some tribal leaders have opened up the land to gambling casinos, which has had a detrimental effect on local communities. Meanwhile many Native communities are still suffering from the aftermath of centuries of persecution and abuse, with high levels of alcoholism, drug addiction, and broken families. The struggle to rebuild self-respect for Native Americans still has a long way to go, and while the wider North American culture is now more positive about such traditions, it still carries a legacy of past attitudes and problems.

SELF-GOVERNMENT IN CANADA

Self-government is also an issue in Canada, where similar political and economic opportunities for Native peoples have been even slower to arrive than in the United States. Following the confrontation between the Mohawk and the Canadian Army in 1990, the Mohawk people negotiated with the government in the difficult work that led to the establishment of the 633 self-governing reservations in 1996. Because many of these reservations are extremely small, they still have difficulty exerting real political power. Yet they have the assurance that the law gives them the grounds to do so.

Where land has been returned to Canadian tribes, these tribes have demonstrated an ability to manage it successfully. The Inuk people of northern Quebec, who reclaimed their territory in a 1975 settlement, now run local airlines and have built several meatpacking factories.

NATIVE AMERICANS AND THE ENVIRONMENTAL MOVEMENT

The environmental movement of the 1970s, along with the other political actions, also helped draw attention to Native American attitudes, particularly the Native Americans' closeness to animals, plants, and the land. A sympathetic alliance sprang up between some Native American spiritual leaders and those environmentalists who were interested in protecting the Earth and its resources. Environmentalists considered the land and its natural inhabitants to be worthy of conservation; from this perspective they were in agreement with the Native Americans.

Environmentalists promoted interest in Indian attitudes toward the land and made people aware of the respect Native Americans had for the Earth they inhabited. However, the land and the plants and animals that inhabit it are sacred to Native Americans in a deeply religious sense. To Native Americans, for example, an eagle is not only an endangered species; it is a sacred being that commands reverential respect even if it were not endangered. Though they recognized Native American respect for the land and its resources, environmentalists often missed the more religious roots of those convictions.

NATIVE AMERICAN RELIGIONS AND MODERN SOCIETY

The issue of religious concern for a sacred environment suggests broader areas of tension between the theoretical positions of Native American religions and the actual life Native Americans pursue within modern North American society. Being an

Indian in North American society does not necessarily guarantee that one is a Native American who has retrieved one's religious roots.

Native religions were strong largely because they were practiced in small, tightly knit communities. People lived in close quarters; they knew each other almost as members of a family. These extended families took responsibility for each other as brothers and sisters. However, when Native Americans moved to cities, community commitments were dissolved. Furthermore Native Americans were attached to their sacred lands as an essential part of Native worship. Because cities had no such lands, urban Native Americans were cut off from the wellspring of their religious life.

RESTORED TO LAND

When the U.S. government forced Native Americans onto reservations, there was certainly a basis for some resentment. Native Americans opposed governmental interference in their lives. They also were not always happy with the lands chosen to be their reservations. At times these lands were simply locations unwanted by others. However, from a religious perspective, the lands denied to them often were lands that they considered sacred. Nonetheless, the restoration of the lands they did acquire was, from a religious viewpoint, a saving factor. Simply being restored to land gave Native Americans the opportunity to renew their religious appreciation of the Earth, even if it was not always the Earth they had previously worshipped.

FINDING MUTUAL UNDERSTANDING

Today many Native Americans have grown up as Christians. Their families may have converted at a time when it was against the laws of their country to practice traditional Indian religious rituals. Or, more positively, they may have found that certain forms of Christianity could in some way accommodate their own Native beliefs and practices. It is often very difficult to flesh out the differences between viewing the world as God's creation and viewing the world as a sacred realm of the gods. There are certainly differences, but many Christians and Native Americans today wrestle with those differences within a context of attempted mutual understanding.

NATIVE AMERICAN RELIGIONS AND POPULAR CULTURE

Native American thought and belief has gained the attention of many non-Indians searching for spiritual meaning. In the minds of some Native Americans, however, popularity is in itself also a problem. They point out that their religion is a way of life, a habit of thought acquired over a lifetime. It is not something that can be picked up in a class or from reading a book.

For people who are not well informed, it can be difficult to tell the difference between a true Native American spiritual healer and a popular fraud. Traditional Native American spiritual leaders scorn individuals who endeavor to trade on Native American

Children playing outside their home on a Navajo reservation in Utah. Increasingly the legal right to self-government is being recognized by the federal government, but traditional lands are not being officially recognized as sacred land. Although Native American lands may be protected, this is often because they happen to be in official wilderness areas.

spirituality by calling themselves healers and by claiming to pass on traditional ancient secrets.

There are strong reasons for many Native American spiritual leaders to hesitate to work with non-Native Americans or even to include them in rituals for renewal or healing. It is easy to understand, then, why the complex efforts at interreligious dialogue leave Native Americans confused. They have not fully resolved questions of whether their practice of religion should include outsiders or not. Many believe that the holiest of rituals should belong only to tribal members. Outside participants can follow all the nonliturgical or communal movements, but it is very difficult for them to share fully the spiritual mysteries involved.

CONTINUING TENSIONS

Cultural differences between the governments of the United States and Canada and the Native American tribes, as well as between states or provinces where Native tribes are located, still create tensions. A tribe might stir up controversy by setting up a building where items are sold but no state taxes are collected. The tribe is exempt from taxes, but such tax-exempt sales undermine other non-tax-exempt businesses in the area and undercut state tax revenues. A crisis could develop, especially in a time of a state or provincial tax crisis. These cases seem to be purely financial matters, but other issues might challenge the legal systems more seriously.

The Native American Church claimed exemption from U.S. drug laws, at least in the particular cases of peyote rituals of the Half-Moon Ceremony and Kiowa Way. For ordinary American citizens peyote was a drug; for the members of the Native American Church it was a sacrament. In the judgment of Native Americans peyote should be considered in a way parallel to Christian sacraments.

SACRED LAND

It is very difficult to grasp the significance of "sacred land" for Native Americans. It is even hard for government officials and judges to understand this concept. In general when we think of land we usually divide it into two types—developed or undeveloped. Developed land is land that has been set aside for designated uses: for housing, businesses, roads, farms, and other enterprises. Undeveloped land is viewed as areas that are sheltered for various reasons: for the protection of wildlife, the preservation of places of special natural beauty, and other humane concerns. *Wilderness* is the name we usually give to such undeveloped regions. For Native Americans, however, *sacred land* is not really a synonym for *wilderness.* For them a traditional tribal burial site is a religious or sacred burial place. It is the land of their ancestral gods. Such a site is not a preserve that can be moved or altered for purely human considerations.

THE ISSUE OF "WILDERNESS LAND"

In 1988 the claim of the Native Americans in northern California to religious rights over a sacred burial place was tested in the Supreme Court in the case of *Lyng v. Northwest Indian Cemetery Protective Association.* The rights of the Native Americans were denied. The court found in favor of the National Forest Service and its plan to build a service road on this land. One of the major arguments in support of this decision was based on the view that the issue was a battle over "wilderness land" and its rights in relation to other needs. The Native American claim to religious or sacred respect for the burial land was passed over as if it was a privately held feeling of Native Americans that had no place in the realm of public concerns.

THE MEANING OF *SACRED LAND*

Such legal decisions underline the fact that *sacred land* has a different meaning for Native Americans than it does for most

RESTORING BLUE LAKE

Blue Lake in New Mexico is the "Garden of Eden" for the Taos people. It is also their final resting place, their "heaven." In 1906 President Theodore Roosevelt made Blue Lake part of the Carson National Forest. The Taos people immediately protested and attempted to get back their sacred land. President Richard Nixon, 65 years later, finally had it restored to them. This is one instance of a successful, though long-delayed, outcome for Native people. Still, many other places, equally sacred, remain as government property and Native American worshippers' access to them is restricted or denied.

other Americans. The result is that, paradoxically, many sacred places have been preserved, but not as Native American religious sites. However, many sacred sites have not been protected, and from the viewpoint of the Native Americans they have been desecrated. Many sacred sites have been taken over because of claims for the need for new roads or hikers' paths, or for lucrative logging, or for the development of motorbike trails. As appeals multiply for new land developments to serve these many interests, challenges to Native American claims to sacred lands will continue to increase.

RESPECTING INDIAN ANCESTORS

Conflicts have arisen not only over sacred lands, but also over the remains of Native Americans. The tensions in this realm exist between the Native peoples and the scientific communities of anthropologists, archaeologists, and geneticists. A report

A sign stands in front of Bear Butte, an outcrop that juts above the prairie in South Dakota where some Native Americans hold prayers and religious ceremonies. The State governor, Mike Rounds, wants to spend more than $1 million to prevent developers from putting biker bars and other noisy businesses on ranch land near Bear Butte, which is held sacred by many Native American tribes.

from the Department of the Interior, in 1979, well formulated the terms of the conflict: "The prevalent view in the society of applicable disciplines is that Native American human remains are public property and artifacts for study, display, and cultural investment. It is understandable that this view is in conflict with and repugnant to those Native people whose ancestors and near relatives are considered the property at issue." Native Americans find it ironic that most Americans would be horrified to have their own dead ancestors used for scientific experiments or displayed in museums as educational exhibits, and yet that they do not have the same sensibility in regard to the ancestors of Native Americans.

In the 1980s it was estimated that hundreds of thousands of dead bodies had been taken from Indian graves and battlefields. Statutes against grave robbing in all states seemed seldom to be applied in cases of the Indian dead. In 1990 Congress approved the Native American Graves Protection and Repatriation Act (NAGPRA). It was an attempt on the part of the federal government to give Native tribes control over human skeletons found on federal or tribal lands. This act further provides that museums and other institutions must return such remains for reburial if the tribes from whose land they came request it.

PROTECTING SACRED OBJECTS

In addition to the hundreds of thousands of dead bodies taken from Indian graves, there are millions of ceremonial and cultural objects that have been dug up for relocation in museums or museum storage. NAGPRA also prohibited objects from being considered archaeological resources, forbade any disturbance of sites without tribal consent, and imposed penalties for unauthorized excavation, removal, damage, or destruction. Still, many sacred objects such as medicine masks and fetishes have made their way into museums to be displayed as curiosities.

Museums, universities, and cultural institutes have often been slow to comply with NAGPRA's demands. They have also at times set up conditions for the return of sacred objects, demanding, for example, the same insurance protection that these precious objects had been given in their scientific locations.

One of the more successful efforts at retrieval has been the case of the Zuni Twin War God fetishes. More than 80 of these figures have been returned to the Zuni tribe, and the Zuni continue to search for others in museums and private collections. Their success has encouraged other tribes to pursue efforts to retrieve the sacred relics of their past through legal routes.

THE EAGLE SPIRIT MESSENGER

Eagle feathers are special among all the sacred objects of Native Americans. Just as angels are intermediaries between God and humankind for people of the Bible, so for more than 200 Native American tribes the eagle is the spirit messenger between the Great Spirit and the Earth. Individual tribes have special ceremonies related to the eagle. The Iroquois celebrate their Eagle Dance with traditional songs and dances. At first these were war and peace ceremonies, but today they have become medicine dances. During these rites each person is assigned a ceremonial friend: The friend's role is to provide mutual help in dealing with life's difficulties.

SACRED EAGLE FEATHERS

Though Native Americans view eagle feathers as sacred objects, others, including the government, see eagles as an endangered species and attempt to protect them by law. They consider the killing of eagles to be a crime. Since they presume that those with eagle feathers have gotten them by breaking the law, they consider that those who possess or sell feathers,

> ### The Native Way Is to Pray
>
> *This is the Native way: all of us are related to everything else, to the elements, to all the animal life. We're all connected to the tree life, too—you name it. We're all the same. We're all a part of the water, too—some of us don't realize it, but we are. We are part of the air, and we are part of the fire.*
>
> *We're part of everything here on Earth, and we're part of the Moon, Sun, and stars. We're all connected together here. Indian people always pray to all those things so that they keep moving in the right direction, so that they'll keep us nice and clean, and so we can have a healthier life. That's what we are saying to all those things in our prayers.*
>
> *The Native way is to pray for everything.*
>
> —Corbin Harney, spiritual leader, Western Shoshone Nation.
>
> (In Corbin Harvey, *The Way It Is.*)

even for religious purposes, are guilty of a crime. In 1994 President Clinton signed a directive that made it easier for Native Americans to obtain, for religious purposes, dead eagles found on government lands. Since then eagles have been promptly shipped to the National Eagle Repository, where Native Americans can obtain them on request for religious ceremonies.

THE CHALLENGE TO NATIVE AMERICAN RELIGIONS

There are many challenges to Native American religions. The biggest challenges, perhaps, are facing the ignorance on the part of almost all Americans of the Native American sense of what is sacred and the loss of confidence in their own value among many dispossessed Native American peoples and individuals.

The problem over the notion of the sacred is evident in any consideration of sacred lands, the sacred remains of ancestors, and sacred objects. It seems that some progress has been made in the recovery of some sacred lands, some human remains, and other sacred objects. Laws and executive directives have given some promise of recovery in these religious areas. Yet these laws and directives seem always to miss the heart of the matter. Their authors seem afraid to expand the concept of religion and the "sacred" beyond definitions that fit Western views of religion.

Loss of confidence and self-esteem and the difficulties of finding a clear role within the wider culture are reflected in the levels of family and community breakdown among peoples of Native American descent. Romanticizing the tradition has also been a problem because it has usually been a projection of wishful thinking by non-Native peoples onto Native Americans. This has meant that certain deep-seated problems of authority and identity have not been properly acknowledged.

However, in comparison with the situation even 50 years ago, the place of Native Americans within society is now much more deeply understood, much more profoundly appreciated, and increasingly seen as part of the pluralistic matrix that makes up North American society today.

FACT FILE

Worldwide Numbers
There are approximately 2.8 million people living in the United States and 1.2 million living in Canada who identifiy themselves as Native Americans.

Holy Symbol
The high-flying bald eagle embodies a strong spiritual presence and link between Earth and Heaven. The eagle's feathers are used ritually by many Native American tribes to invoke the bird's spiritual powers.

Holy Writings
Native American religions are based on oral traditions: There are no specific holy writings.

Holy Places
There are no specific pilgrimage sites.

Founders
There is no specific founder of Native American religions.

Festivals
Many tribes follow a calendar of ceremonies that celebrate the renewal of the Earth. They are mostly related to the seasons, migrations of wildlife, or movements of the Moon, Sun and stars.

BIBLIOGRAPHY

Beck, Peggy V. *Sacred: Ways of Knowledge, Sources of Life.* Tsaile, Ariz.: Dine College Press, 2004.

Bierhorst, John. *A Cry from the Earth: Music of the North American Indians.* Santa Fe, N. Mex.: Ancient City Press, 1979.

Bierhorst, John. *In the Trail of the Wind: American Indian Poems and Ritual Orations.* New York: Farrar, Straus, and Giroux, 1998.

Black Elk, Joseph Epes Brown, and Michael F. Steltenkamp. *The Sacred Pipe: Black Elk's Account of the Seven Rites of the Ogalala Sioux.* New York: MJF Books, 1996.

Demetracopoulou, Dorothy. *Wintu Songs.* Berkeley, Calif.: California Indian Library Collections Project, 1989.

Harney, Corbin. *The Way It Is.* Nevada City, Calif.: Blue Dolphin Publishing, 1995.

Joe, Eugene Baatsoslanii, Mark Bahti, and Oscar T. Branson. *Navajo Sandpainting Art.* Tucson: Treasure Chest Publications, 1978.

The United Methodist Hymnal, Nashville, Tenn.: The United Methodist Publishing House, 1989.

Velie, Alan R. *American Indian Literature: An Anthology.* Norman, Okla.: University of Oklahoma Press, 1991.

FURTHER READING

American Indians: Cycles of Life. Alexandria, Va.: Time Life Books, 1999.

American Indians: Spirit World. Alexandria, Va.: Time Life Books, 1999.

Brown, Joseph Epes, and Emily Cousins. *Teaching Spirits: Understanding Native American Religious Traditions.* New York: Oxford University Press, 2001.

Crawford, Suzanne. *Native American Religious Traditions.* Upper Saddle River, N. J.: Prentice Hall, 2006.

DeLoria, Jr., Vine. *God Is Red: A Native View of Religion,* 2nd ed. Golden, Colo.: North American Press, 2003.

Dooling, D. M., and Paul Jordan-Smith. *I Become Part of It: Sacred Dimensions in Native American Life.* New York: Parabola Books, 2002.

Gill, Sam. *Native American Religions: An Introduction,* 2nd ed. Belmont, Calif.: Wadsworth Publishing, 2004.

Harney, Corbin. *The Way It Is.* Nevada City, Calif.: Blue Dolphin Publishing, 1995.

Verslius, Arthur. *Native American Traditions.* Shaftsbury, Dorset, England, and Rockport, Mass.: Element Books, 1994.

WEB SITES

Further facts and figures, history, and current status of the religion can be found on the following Web sites:

http://www.nativeamericans.com/Religion.htm
A Web site providing links to all aspects of Native American religions, cultures, traditions, and beliefs.

http://www.nmai.si.edu/
The Web site of the Smithsonian Institution's National Museum of the American Indian, which deals with all aspects of Native Americans.

http://www.native-languages.org/religion.htm
Provides links to information about Native American languages and religions.

http://en.wikipedia.org/wiki/Native_American_religion
An encyclopedic summary of Native American religions, with links to many specific Web sites.

GLOSSARY

Blessingway—A Navajo ritual for restoring harmony to the Earth, conducted both separately and as a segment of healing rituals.

Buffalo Calf Woman—A representative of the Buffalo People, messengers of the Great Spirit, who brought the sacred pipe to the Lakota so that they might use it to do only good things—make peace between warring nations and heal the sick.

Canku Luta—Lakota Pipe religion.

Changing Woman—Heavenly being to whom the Navajo trace their origins, who created corn and made Earth People; mother of twin sons, who lived with their father, the Sun, who gave them special knowledge and powerful weapons for doing good.

chantways—Navajo rituals for creating balance and harmony or for healing, lasting from one to nine days.

Coyote—A half-animal, half-human being who appears in the tales of many cultures as a trickster/creator.

culture hero—A supernatural being with creative powers, having human or animal form, who created the world, made it ready for humans, and taught the First People how to live on the Earth.

Diyin Diné—Navajo Holy People, including First Man and First Woman, who emerged from a succession of underworlds to prepare the Earth for humankind.

emergence tales—Sacred stories in which people are not created but emerge from the underworld or some other place, such as the bottom of a lake or a clamshell.

encomienda—A 16th-century system under which Spanish colonists forced Native people to work for nothing and to pay them taxes.

gan—Apache mountain spirits similar to Hopi kachinas and Navajo *yei*.

Ghost Shirt—A buckskin garment decorated with symbols, believed to protect the wearer from bullets.

Great Mystery—The Great Spirit; the power underlying all creation.

Green Corn Dance—A ceremony shared by many agricultural peoples to give thanks to the Creator for the year's bounty, and to pray for rain, the well-being of the people, and bountiful harvests.

guardian spirits—Spirit helpers, usually acquired in a dream or vision, that help shamans and other individuals contact higher powers.

ha'athali—Navajo holy person or singer.

hozho—(Navajo) harmony, a state of being in balance with the forces of nature.

Hunkapi—(Lakota) "making of relatives" ceremony.

Inikagapi—(Lakota) the sweat lodge ceremony.

kachina—An ancestral spirit venerated by some southwestern tribes and represented by costumes and masks with symbols of Earth, sky, atmosphere, plants, and animals; a carved representation of a particular spirit.

kiva—Sacred ceremonial chamber of the Hopi and other southwestern tribes.

Koshare and Kurena—Pueblo spirit beings who taught the people how to make crops grow.

Manitou—(Algonquin) Great Spirit or Great Mystery.

medicine bundle—A collection of objects with sacred significance and spirit power, wrapped in an animal skin or in cloth. Medicine bundles are considered to be holy, living things.

medicine lodge—A sacred building representing the universe, in which rituals are conducted by the Algonquin.

medicine man/woman—A shaman, someone with connections to the spirit world and special powers such as curing or foretelling the future.

medicine society—In northeastern tribes, an organization of people who pass through levels of mastery to learn tribal lore, healing rituals, sacred songs, and other sacred knowledge.

Mitakuye' Oyasin—(Lakota) A phrase meaning "All of creation are my relatives," traditionally spoken during a healing ceremony.

object intrusion—A cause of illness in which a foreign object, such as a stone or a bone, is believed to have entered a person's body.

Orenda—(Iroquois) the Great Spirit or Great Mystery.

paho—Prayer sticks made by the Pueblo and left in sacred places to convey prayers to the spirit world.

personate—To represent in material form the spirit whose costume or mask a sacred dancer wears, thus allowing that spirit to enter into the body of the dancer and link the human and supernatural worlds.

peyote—Fruit of a southwestern cactus; a mild hallucinogen, or drug that alters consciousness, used ritually by members of the Native American Church.

poeh—(Tewa) the path of life walked by the first ancestors.

potlatch—A ceremonial feast and giveaway held by Northwest Coast tribes to celebrate any major occasion that includes a ceremonial rite, such as a wedding.

puberty rite—A ritual celebrating a girl's reaching womanhood.

sacred clowns—Dancers who, by their clownlike antics, represent the foolishness of humankind and provoke amusement and laughter during sacred dances.

shaman—A person with a special calling that enables him or her to contact the spirit world for healing and other spiritual purposes. Also called medicine man or medicine woman, singer, and other names.

singer—Navajo name for a holy person or religious leader.

Sky Woman—Heavenly being to whom the Iroquois and neighboring tribes trace their origins; mother of twin sons who are considered the creators of the world as humans know it.

soul loss—A cause of illness in which evil spirits capture a sick person's soul and carry it to the underworld.

spirit—The life, or breath, in all natural things, including sky beings: Sun, Moon, and stars; spirits of the atmosphere: rain and wind; animal and plant spirits; powers of the underworld; and the spirits of the dead.

Sun Dance—A complex of rituals and dances performed by Plains tribes for world renewal, usually performed over four days.

sweat lodge ceremony—A form of ritual purification that precedes all important ceremonies and is conducted separately for health and healing, practiced widely by Native Americans.

taboo—A forbidden act; breaking a taboo can cause misfortune to an individual or a tribe.

Tijus-keha—Iroquois culture hero, Master of Life, son of Sky Woman, and twin to Tawis-karong, whose creations were evil.

trickster—A supernatural being who plays practical jokes, breaks taboos, spoils the works of the culture hero, or otherwise makes trouble.

vision quest—A period of fasting, prayer, and isolation in a sacred place, during which a person may acquire a guardian spirit or spiritual guidance.

Wakan Tanka—(Lakota) the Great Spirit or Great Mystery.

wapiye' win—(Lakota) a medicine woman or "spirit-calling woman."

water-pouring ritual—Tewa ritual conducted when a child is about 10 years old to mark his or her passage into adulthood.

world renewal—Ceremonies performed annually for maintaining order and harmony in the world.

yei—A symbolic figure of the holy people who represent the higher forces of the Navajo universe.

INDEX

A

Algonquin, 20, 36–37, 84
animal dances 59–60
animal spirits 24, 25–26, 36;
    fetishes 79; and sweat lodge
    ceremonies 65
Anishinabe (Chippewa) 79
Apache: healing rituals 79;
    puberty rites 94–96
Arapaho 66–69

B

Buffalo Calf Woman 8, 25, 30,
    52–54, 92

C

ceremonies 15; dances 8, 10,
    56–61, 65–69, 113, 117-
    120; for healing 79–84;
    music for 61–63; naming
    ceremonies 88–91; sacred
    clowns 71; sacred objects
    29–30; the secret rites 52;
    summer solstice 72; sweat
    lodge ceremony 63–65;
    tobacco and 27; winter sol-
    stice 71–72; world renewal
    ceremonies 65 See also rites
    of passage
Changing Woman 45–47, 96
chantways 82–84
Cherokee 17–18; animal spirits
    26; herbalism 85; and ill-
    ness 76
Cheyenne 66–69
children: childhood rituals
    91–93; naming ceremonies
    88–91; puberty rites 93–97
Christianity 13, 27, 40–41, 100–
    101, 104–123, 130–131
Corn Dance 58, 59, 69–70
costumes 58–59, 60–61, 72
Coyote 48

creation stories 17, 24, 41–55
Creator 23, 50–51
Crow 27

D

dance 30, 59, 65–70, 72, 113,
    117–120
death 98–101
Diyin Diné ("Holy People")
    44–45
dreams 15, 23 See also visions

E

eagle dances 59–60
eagle feathers 136–137
education 116–117
ethics 13, 51

F

fasting 66–67
female shamans 33–34, 79
flesh piercing 66
funerals 98–101

G

Ghost Dance 117–120
Great Spirit 15, 19, 22–23;
    communion with 27; and
    plants 26
guardian spirits 34–37

H

Haida: naming ceremonies 90;
    Raven 48–49
Handsome Lake (Skaniadariio)
    109–110
healers and healing 32, 33,
    74–87
Hopi 18; childhood rituals
    92–93; kachina costumes
    60–61; masks and 30; nam-
    ing ceremonies 90; reserva-
    tions 113; wedding ritual

98; the winter and summer
    solstice 71–72
Hunkapi ceremony 92
Huron 30

I

illness and healing 74–87
Indian Shaker Church 115–116
Inuit 18; animal dances 60;
    guardian spirits 36–37;
    Raven 48–49; shaman 33
Iroquoi: Corn Dance 69; and
    illness 76; and missionaries
    109–110; Orenda (Great
    Spirit) 20; Sky Woman
    41–44; tricksters 47

K

kachina costumes 60–61, 72
Kwakiutl, the: dances 58; nam-
    ing ceremonies 90

L

Lakota: animal spirits 25; Buf-
    falo Calf Woman 52–54;
    childhood rituals 92; female
    shamans 34, 79; flesh
    piercing 66; healing rituals
    79, 80–82; and music 61;
    puberty rites 97; sacred
    clowns 71; sacred pipe
    30, 52–54; sacred rites 52;
    Sitting Bull 119–120; Sun
    Dance 8, 12, 66–69; sweat
    lodge ceremony 63–65;
    tricksters 47; Wakan Tanka
    (Great Spirit) 20, 22, 52
Luiseño: and the sky spirits 24;
    tricksters 47

M

marriage 97–98
masks 30, 58–59

ABOUT THE AUTHOR

The late **Paula R. Hartz** was a teacher and a textbook editor, and specialized in writing nonfiction and educational materials for elementary and secondary school students. She is the author of *Baha'i Faith, Daoism, Native American Religions, Taoism,* and *Zoroastrianism,* all from Chelsea House's World Religions series.

ABOUT THE SERIES EDITORS

Martin Palmer is the founder of ICOREC (International Consultancy on Religion, Education, and Culture) in 1983 and is the secretary-general of the Alliance of Religions and Conservation (ARC). He is the author of many books on world religions.

Joanne O'Brien has an M.A. degree in theology and has written a range of educational and general reference books on religion and contemporary culture. She is co-author, with Martin Palmer and Elizabeth Breuilly, of *Religions of the World* and *Festivals of the World* published by Facts On File Inc.

PICTURE CREDITS

Title Page: © iStockphoto.com/Ronnie Wilson; Table of Contents: © iStockphoto.com/Kaye Kerr; Pages 8–9: © Robert van der Hilst/CORBIS; 14: © iStockphoto.com/Frank Leung; 16: © iStockphoto.com/Alexey Stiop; 18: © TopFoto/ImageWorks; 20–21: © iStockphoto.com/Jeremy Edwards; 22: © iStockphoto.com/Doak Heyser; 25: © iStockphoto.com/Chris Pritchard; 28: © TopFoto/Fortean; 29: © iStockphoto.com/Joe Carter; 31: © iStockphoto.com/thumb; 33: © iStockphoto.com/Paul Tessier; 35: © iStockphoto.com/ZiMa; 38–39: © National Geographic/Getty Images; 40: © iStockphoto.com/Jeremy Edwards; 43: © Topham Picturepoint; 49: © www.shutterstock.com/kavram; 50: © iStockphoto.com/Bruce Block; 53: © Denver Public Library, Western History Collection (David Frances Barry); 55: © TopFoto/ImageWorks; 56–57: © Nancy Carter/North Wind Picture Archives; 59: © www.shutterstock.com/Ryan Morgan; 60: © The British Museum/HIP/Topfoto; 63: © Mike Greenlar/The Image Works/Topfoto; 64: © TopFoto/ImageWorks; 67: © World History Archive/Topfoto; 68: © Nancy Carter/North Wind Picture Archives; 74–75: © Nancy Carter/North Wind Picture Archives; 77: © iStockphoto.com/Loretta Hostettler; 78: © Library of Congress (ppmsc 02441); 81: © Werner Forman Archive/Schindler Collection, New York; 83: © Nancy Carter/North Wind Picture Archives; 88–89: © Willard R. Culver/National Geographic/Getty Images; 92: © iStockphoto.com/Steven Allan; 94: © Corbis; 99: © iStockphoto.com/Norman Eder; 101: © iStockphoto.com/Andrew Penner; 102–103: © iStockphoto.com/Nancy Nehring; 105: © AP Photo/Christopher Fitzgerald; 108: © iStockphoto.com/ Specular Photo of Dallas; 111: © North Wind Picture Archives; 114: © Denver Public Library, Colorado Historical Society, and Denver Art Museum; 117: © Denver Public Library, Western History Collection; 118: © Denver Public Library, Western History Collection; 122: © AP Photo; 124–125: © AP Photo/Matt York; 126: © AP Photo/Joe Cavaretta; 131: © TopFoto/ImageWorks; 136: © AP Photo/Morry Gash.